WAYNESBURG COLLEGE LIBRARY
WAYNESBURG, PA.

W9-CKS-249

K95t

809.915

Kugel, James L.
AUTHOR
The Techniques of Strangeness in
TITLE

809.915   K95t
Kugel, James L.
The Techniques of Strangeness in Symbolist
Poetry
91762

MAR 20 72

DISCARDED

The Techniques of Strangeness in Symbolist Poetry

THE TECHNIQUES OF STRANGENESS

IN SYMBOLIST POETRY

by James L. Kugel

New Haven and London, Yale University Press

1971

Published with assistance from the
Louis Effingham deForest Memorial Fund.

Copyright © 1971 by Yale University.
All rights reserved. This book may not be
reproduced, in whole or in part, in any form
(except by reviewers for the public press),
without written permission from the publishers.
Library of Congress catalog card number: 77-118729
International standard book number: 0-300-01352-3

Designed by John O. C. McCrillis
and set in Times Roman type.
Printed in the United States of America by
The Vail-Ballou Press, Inc., Binghamton, New York.

Distributed in Great Britain, Europe, and Africa by
Yale University Press, Ltd., London; in Canada by
McGill-Queen's University Press, Montreal; in Mexico
by Centro Interamericano de Libros Académicos,
Mexico City; in Central and South America by Kaiman &
Polon, Inc., New York City; in Australasia by Australia
and New Zealand Book Co., Pty., Ltd., Artarmon, New
South Wales; in India by UBS Publishers' Distributors Pvt.,
Ltd., Delhi; in Japan by John Weatherhill, Inc.,
Tokyo.

Quotations from "John Wesley Harding" and
"All Along the Watchtower," by Bob Dylan,
copyright © 1968 by Dwarf Music, Inc. Used
by permission of Dwarf Music, Inc.

489

1301 /

8.4911 /

91762

For my grandfather Samuel Roth,
poet and publisher, who first read
modern poetry to me.

Contents

Acknowledgments

I would like to thank the many people whose help has contributed to this book. I am first of all indebted to the inexhaustible patience and perseverance of Professor A. B. Giamatti, who supervised the research and writing and without whom the book could never have appeared in print. I would like to thank as well Professors René Wellek and Victor Ehlich for their help on several sections, and Professor Tsvetan Todorov for his suggestions. My thanks also go to John Jagodzinski for his comments, and to many friends who have read through the manuscript. Finally, let me thank Wayland Schmitt and Barbara Folsom of Yale Press for their help with the rewriting and processing of the manuscript.

A Note on Translations: I have left passages in French untranslated, assuming that most readers will be able to get along on their own. Russian prose extracts all appear in translation only; Russian poems have been printed in the original, along with preexistent translations where possible. Where translations of Russian poems were unavailable or inadequate, I have provided my own English paraphrase.

1. What Is Symbolism?

Early in 1968 Bob Dylan—already nationally famous as a singer and lyricist—brought out a new record album, *John Wesley Harding*. Prior to that time I had not listened closely to Dylan's records, enjoying the music and not paying very much attention to the words. But one afternoon shortly after this new album was released I had a chance to listen to it carefully several times over, and I immediately noticed phrases and even whole songs that reminded me of the style of some of the Symbolist poetry I had recently read. This particular collection of songs by Dylan was surprisingly reminiscent of *Douze Chansons,* a booklet of verse published by Maurice Maeterlinck in 1896 and which I had read only a few weeks previous.

Both the album and the booklet consist primarily of ballads (the latter exclusively so)—strange, mysterious narratives that seem to be played out in some remote time and locale. Both are characterized by tight, simple-sounding language, and the songs are full of storybook characters: kings and queens, beggars and blind men. One baffling aspect of these ballads is that, while they appear to be describing some event or happening, exactly what is being described is never quite clear. Even when the narration does seem to be taking some shape, the reader or listener is completely ignorant of what motivates the characters, and hence the actions described lack an understandable context. Maeterlinck's book is full of young angels and sisters who are simply waiting—we don't know what for—or who go somewhere and never come back—we don't know why. Dylan's events are similarly elusive. In the title song he describes an exploit of John Wesley Harding, a kind of gun-toting mythic hero who, among other virtues, "was never known to hurt an honest man." Each of the song's three stanzas ends with a similar line praising one of the hero's good qualities, but the relationship of such praise to the rest of the song is never too clear. Furthermore, events in the song tend

1

to be alluded to but never stated outright. Thus the incident
which is the song's subject is set forth in the second stanza:

> It was down in Cheney County,
> The time they talk about;
> With his lady by his side he took a stand;
> And soon the situation there
> Was all but straightened out:
> He was always known to lend a helping hand.

This is supposedly the central action of the poem—one that,
we learn in the next stanza, has made the telegraph wires
hum with excitement. But what happened?

This is a typical Dylan twist, and it is most striking in his
"All Along the Watchtower" in the same album:

> "There must be some way out of here,"
> Said the joker to the thief,
> "There's too much confusion,
> I can't get no relief.
> Businessmen they drink my wine
> Ploughmen dig my earth,
> None of them along the line
> Know what any of it is worth."
>
> "No reason to get excited,"
> The thief he kindly spoke,
> "There are many here among us
> Who feel life is but a joke.
> But you and I we've been through that,
> And this is not our fate,
> So let us not talk falsely now,
> The hour is getting late . . ."
>
> All along the watchtower
> Princes kept the view
> While all the women came and went,
> Their footservants too.
> Outside in the distance

> A wildcat did growl.
> Two riders were approaching.
> The wind began to howl.

The listener does not have a very clear idea about where the first two stanzas are being spoken, but there is an implication ("There are many here among us") that the "joker" and the "thief"—two storybook characters—belong to a larger group of people massed together somewhere. One might suspect that the opening line, "There must be some way out of here," implies a prison camp of some sort, but it may only be a figurative prison, an inextricable situation of the spirit. In any case, both joker and thief feel oppressed and taken advantage of, and both—refusing to accept the absurdity of it ("life is but a joke," etc.)—seem to agree that action is necessary: "The hour is getting late."

The scene then changes to a fairy-tale landscape, with a watchtower and, perhaps, a castle. There is a postulated wilderness nearby, for a wildcat growls ominously. The shift from the first two stanzas to the third is so abrupt that it seems to deny any real connection. At the same time, the fact that all three stanzas belong to the same song implies there must be some relationship between them. At this point the two riders appear, and they present a possible resolution. The two riders are (or, to be faithful to the listener's own hesitancy, *seem* to be) none other than the joker and the thief who, having resolved to act, are moving toward the tower. The wind howls ominously. What is going to happen? What is the connection between the pair's grievances and the people of the tower? What of the dissonance between "businessmen," a modern-sounding word, and the whole courtly company described in the third stanza? In short, what is the nature of the action described in the poem?

Before discussing these questions, I would like to turn to the other singer under examination, Maurice Maeterlinck, and to consider a song of his that strikes me as being similar in method to Dylan's ballad.

Elle est Venue vers le Palais

Elle est venue vers le palais
—Le soleil se levait à peine—
Elle est venue vers le palais
Les chevaliers se regardaient
Toutes les femmes se taisaient.

Elle s'arrêta devant la porte
—Le soleil se levait à peine—
Elle s'arrêta devant la porte
On entendit marcher la reine
Et son époux l'interrogeait.

Où allez-vous, où allez-vous?
—Prenez garde, on y voit à peine—
Où allez-vous, où allez-vous?
Quelqu'un vous attend-il là-bas?
Mais elle ne répondait pas.

Elle descendit vers l'inconnue
—Prenez garde, on y voit à peine—
Elle descendit vers l'inconnue
L'inconnue embrassa la reine
Elles ne se dîrent pas un mot
Et s'éloignèrent aussitôt.

Son époux pleurait sur le seuil
—Prenez garde, on y voit à peine—
Son époux pleurait sur le seuil
On entendait marcher la reine
On entendait tomber les feuilles.[1]

Maeterlinck presents another mysterious action. An "unknown woman"—who nevertheless seems to be recognized by the knights and ladies (or is it that her appearance is so particularly striking?)—approaches the palace. It is daybreak. By the time the lady visitor is at the gates, the queen is readying herself to meet her, and the king is clearly disturbed by

---

1. M. Maeterlinck, *Poésies Complètes*, pp. 195-96.

what is going on. The queen, having failed to answer her husband's question, ("Where are you going? Where are you going?"), goes downstairs to meet the woman; they embrace and, without exchanging a word, part and go their separate ways. The king weeps: Is it because his wife did not answer him, or because there is something about her going to meet the unknown stranger that has brought him some unexplained grief? The queen is pacing as before, and the leaves fall ominously in the background.

This ominous conclusion fulfills a role comparable to that of the howling wind in Dylan's ballad, but the similarity between the two poems is not limited to their last lines. In both, we are presented with a sketchy sort of action playing itself out in a remote, fairy-tale setting. In both, the characters are rather undefined, identified, for the most part, only by "type" or occupational titles (joker, thief, king, queen, princes, ladies). Most important, the action that does take place is enveloped in *implied significance*—a wildcat growls, the wind howls, glances are exchanged, the king weeps, the leaves fall —and yet, the significance of these occurrences cannot quite be grasped. What is so important about the riders' approach or the unknown woman's visit may be subject to speculation, but cannot be known. What the poems do, then, is provide a direction for the reader's imagination without offering it a means of satisfaction. These are not parables, nor are they allegories; perhaps the most we can say is that they are models of a thought situation, invented archetypes which, however they may resound in the reader's consciousness, leave him with the feeling of having witnessed something mysterious and utterly strange.

These two poems have within them the seeds of the two central ideas discussed in the present study. The first, briefly stated, is this: that the mysteriousness of both poems is a peculiarly Symbolist phenomenon—that, in fact, after seventy-five years of this kind of verse, what we mean by the term *Symbolism* is this poetic strangeness. To the extent to which poetic techniques can be isolated, then, the techniques of Symbolist poetry can be defined as techniques of strangeness. The second idea is that Dylan and many of the freshest young writers of today represent, not a renaissance of Symbolism in American poetry, but a continuing tradition which began in English as early as the 1890s and has never stopped. And here I am not claiming that all poetry since that time has been Symbolist, but that modern poetry (as other critics have recently claimed) *begins* with the Symbolist movement. More emphatically, we can say this: Symbolism changed our whole notion of what poetry is, changed the reader's expectations in approaching a poem; and that is where modern poetry begins.

Understanding Symbolism and its techniques, then, is an important first step to reading a great many poems written in this century. And to understand it, it is necessary to go back to a small group of poets who wrote in Paris during the days when Romanticism was drawing to a close.

The Symbolist movement began in the late nineteenth century, in the wake of the so-called "Parnassian" (late Romantic) poets. The Symbolists admired some of these late Romantics, but their real heroes were "misfit" writers like Charles Baudelaire, Gérard de Nerval, and Edgar Allan Poe, and their stated aim was not to create "descriptive objectivity" in poetry, as was then the vogue, but to get away from description and "themes" entirely. What the Symbolists wanted was to create "suggestiveness," musicality, and *la poésie pure*— pure poetry.

At first, the Symbolist group centered around a young French poet of Greek origin, Jean Moréas. Later, leadership passed to the poet Stéphane Mallarmé, who surrounded himself with a "school" of younger colleagues, including Gustave Kahn, René Ghil, Henri de Régnier, Albert Samain, and many others. They met regularly on Tuesday evenings in Mallarmé's apartment to read and discuss poetry.

In 1883, Paul Verlaine published *Les Poetes maudits,* a book of brief biographies of the leading Symbolists, and this greatly increased their reputation. By the late 1880s, despite the defection of Moréas and various splinter groups, the Symbolist school had become the rallying point of young poets throughout France, and self-avowed Symbolist periodicals were more and more in evidence. Many poets peripheral to the school began to be associated with it, either in fact or in rumor. Verlaine, who outside of his recent book had had very little to do with the principal Symbolists, was now linked with them, as was (somewhat later, and with better reason) Arthur Rimbaud. Other names became prominent: Tristan Corbière and Jules Laforgue, and the patriarchal figures of Saint-Pol-Roux and Francis Jammes. French Symbolism continued into the twentieth century with Paul Valéry and Paul Claudel.

Perhaps because of the irrefutable appeal of its aesthetic slogans, or the great amount of good writing done in its name, or the promise of a new literary movement in a world where Classicism and Romanticism were already history— perhaps for all these reasons—Symbolism gradually became an international phenomenon. Among the Belgian Symbolists were Emile Verhaeren and Maurice Maeterlinck, in Germany there was a group centered around Stefan George and the *Blätter für die Kunst,* and there were schools in Italy, Spain, and the Slavic countries. But the Russian Symbolists constitute the most important school outside of France—one that involved two generations of major Russian poets: Konstantin Bal'mont, Valerij Brjusov, Vjačeslav Ivanov, Fëdor Sologub, Dmitri Merežkovskij, Zinaida Gippius, Aleksandr Blok, Andrej Belyj and Innokentij Annenskij. Even in countries where no school was founded, such as the United States or Britain, Symbolism found admirers: William Butler Yeats, T. S. Eliot, Ezra Pound, Hart Crane, and Wallace Stevens. At the middle of the twentieth century the effects of the French *école symboliste* were still being felt in many different national literatures.

Such, more or less, is the conventional history of Symbolism as we know it. But the question of what exactly Symbol-

ism was, is not so easily answered as the foregoing summary
might imply: there are quite a few unknowns. For example,
if one tries to define Symbolism historically, to view it as an
event in the history of literature, one runs up against a simple-
sounding but difficult question: When did Symbolism begin
and end? If it is to be defined not in historical but in aesthetic
terms, as an aesthetic system like Classicism or Romanticism,
there is another problem: What exactly was the Symbolist
world-view; how did the Symbolists as a group see art and
life? And if Symbolism is examined from neither of these
standpoints, but simply in terms of the individual poets who
comprise the movement, a third question arises: Who were
they, these "real" Symbolists, as opposed to their non-Symbolist contemporaries? Under close scrutiny, none of these
questions can be answered satisfactorily.

When Did Symbolism Begin and End?

The term *Symbolist* was first used in 1885 by Jean Moréas
in reference to the small school of French poets which he
headed. To him, "Symbolism" meant this school. But to
accept his definition would be to make the history of French
Symbolism extremely brief:

1883	Publication of Verlaine's *Poètes maudits,* sketches of several future Symbolists.
1884	Joris-Karl Huysmans's *A Rebours,* a novel about the prototypical "décadent," mentions Mallarmé; Moréas starts his salon of "symboliques"; Tuesday evening meetings of Mallarmé.
1885	Moréas launches *symbolisme* (leaflets, manifestos).
1885–90	Various competing movements: *le symbolisme* (Mallarmé, Moréas), *les décadents* (Anatole Baju), *l'école instrumentiste* (René Ghil).

1891   Moréas breaks away to found *l'école romane* and Mallarmé takes over leadership of the Symbolists.

by 1895   The Symbolist school begins to wane; younger poets attack its doctrinal excesses.

1898   Death of Mallarmé.

Obviously, to say that Symbolism equals the Symbolist school is too narrow a definition. Since the idea of "school" connotes work done *in concert,* or at least in an awareness of one's colleagues, we would have to eliminate from the Symbolist school Rimbaud (who never met Mallarmé and who had, in fact, stopped writing before Mallarmé published his first book), Isidore Ducasse (Lautréamont), early Verlaine, and others. At the same time, we would disregard all the Symbolists who wrote after Mallarmé's death: Valéry and Claudel in France, and most of the English, Russian, German, Belgian, Italian, and American followers of the French Symbolists.

For historical reasons, treating Symbolism as a "movement" or "period" might seem like an easier notion to deal with, since it dismisses the associative connotations of "school." But where, then, does such a movement start? Most critics would agree that Baudelaire, for example, is to be considered, not a Symbolist, but a common ancestor whom the Symbolists revered, "un vrai dieu!" [2] Does Symbolism, therefore, begin with Rimbaud, who was composing his greatest poetry in 1870? Or perhaps with Ducasse, who had already published *les Chants de Maldoror* in 1869?

Similarly, even if one accepts the idea that "period" implies, not exact dates, but roughly delineated eras with many overlapping spheres, Symbolism's other extreme poses insoluble problems. Although most critics have come to think of a "crise des valeurs symbolistes" at the beginning of the

2. This is Rimbaud's tribute, and it appears in his famous "Lettre du voyant," May 15, 1871, in A. Rimbaud, *Œuvres Complètes,* p. 349.

WAYNESBURG COLLEGE LIBRARY
WAYNESBURG, PA.

twentieth century,[3] such a view runs the risk of equating
Symbolism's dethronement as the dominant literary aesthetic
in France with its cessation pure and simple. This, of course,
is not the case, as Claudel's *Feuilles des Saints* (1924),
Valéry's *La Jeune Parque* (1917) and *Charmes* (1922–26),
and other works attest. (Indeed, Valéry did not stop writing
until the 1940s.) Is Symbolism, then, to span nearly a century, overlapping with Realism, Naturalism, Surrealism, and
lettrisme? And only France is being considered here; if the
Symbolist poets of other literatures are included, the boundaries stretch still farther. Thus the unresolved diffculty remains: How can we deal with Symbolism as a historical
phenomenon if we do not know where it begins or ends?

What Was the Symbolists' Artistic Credo?

My brief overview mentioned some of the catchwords
first popularized by the Symbolists. Rather than description, they claimed to strive for "evocativeness," [4] musicality,[5] mysteriousness,[6] a refusal of rhetoric and the "parler

3. See M. Décaudin, *Crise des valeurs symbolistes,* which views the
history of Symbolism in terms of a series of crises and regroupments.

4. G. Michaud, *La Doctrine symboliste,* presents a summary of
Symbolist pronouncements which led to the general acceptance of
these slogans, and the citations in this and the following four notes
are drawn from his book, pp. 15-78. "Eveiller, c'est le dire de
Mallarmé: 'suggerer, voilà le rêve; c'est le parfait usage de ce mystère
qui constitue le symbole' " (Saint-Antoine, 1894, in Michaud, p. 48).
"Symboliser est èvoquer, non dire, narrer et peindre; la chose n'est
maîtresse que lorsque . . . de par ses qualités seules de rêve et de
suggestion elle renaît et perce la pensée qu'elle devient le voile
volontaire" (René Ghil, 1886, in Michaud, p. 74).

5. The notion is common from the time of Verlaine's famous
poem "Art poétique," which begins "De la Musique avant toute
chose . . ." Cf. T. de Wyzéwa, "La poésie véritable, la seule qui
demeure irréductible à la littérature proprement dite, est une musique
émotionnelle de syllabes et de rythmes" (Michaud, p. 78).

6. "Il doit y avoir toujours énigme en poésie, c'est le but de la
littérature" (Mallarmé, in response to Jules Huret's "Enquête littéraire," 1891; the entire interview is reprinted in S. Mallarmé, *Œuvres
complètes.* "La poésie est l'expression, par le langage humain ramené

relatif," [7] a quest for the absolute, [8] and a theory of universal symbolism, using Baudelaire's *correspondances* as their point of departure. [9] Such terms, however, present a problem of correspondences—not of the Baudelairean kind, but simply correspondences among the views on Symbolist aesthetics held by its various practitioners. In discussing this question the critic A. G. Lehmann wisely abandoned any notion of Symbolism as a unified aesthetic, arguing that concepts such as "symbol" had quite different meanings for Camille Mauclair, René Ghil, Téodor de Wyzewa, François Viélé-Griffin, Gustave Kahn, Mallarmé, and Valéry. [10] Their aesthetic views were, to be sure, formed under the influence of the same aesthetic predecessors; nevertheless, to inflate the common ground of these views into one, all-purpose viewpoint must lead to a definition too general to have meaning as a particularly Symbolist view. The outcome of Lehmann's struggle to find a meaning of "symbol" acceptable to most of the Symbolists is the best proof of this point. He ends up defining "symbol" as "the aesthetic unity of created art, which is indifferently unity of form and unity of content." [11]

à son rythme essentiel, du sens mystérieux des aspects de l'existence" (Mallarmé, 1886, in Michaud, p. 15).

7. "Ennemis [sic] de l'enseignement, la déclamation, la fausse sensibilité, la description objective, la poésie symbolique cherche à vêtir l'Idée d'une forme sensible qui, néanmoins, ne serait pas son but à elle-même, mais qui . . . demeurerait sujette" (Jean Moréas, 1886, in Michaud, p. 25.)

8. As in the single-minded search of the Symbolist hero, discussed later. The same absolutism appears in Symbolist definitions of "symbol": "Le symbole s'épure donc toujours à travers une évocation . . . il ruine toute contingence, tout fait, tout detail; il est la plus haute expression d'art et la plus spiritualiste qui soit" (Emile Verhaeren, 1888, in Michaud, p. 54).

9. Michaud devotes an entire section (pp. 13-42) to this subject.

10. See A. G. Lehmann, *The Symbolist Aesthetic in France, 1885-1895*, p. 271 ff., and Michaud, pp. 43-61.

11. Lehmann, p. 302. My purpose in quoting this definition is to point out that (a) this is a synthetic view and does not represent the intended meaning of the word as it was used by all of Mallarmé's

In fact, on this very question of symbol, we must reaffirm a truth now apparent to many critics: [12] that *Symbolism* (the school, the movement, or the period) must not be confused with *symbolism,* the use of symbols in literature. As to what is meant by the latter there is no small amount of debate and disagreement; but in any case few would argue today that the Symbolists invented symbolism or even did something radically different with it. (That is, whatever the Symbolists' innovation, it is best dealt with in terms other than *symbol.*) With the word *symbol,* as in so many instances, the Symbolists present a united rhetorical front without any real unanimity, and the result is that the term becomes practically meaningless in regard to them.

A further problem of correspondences arises when one compares the French Symbolists' theories to their own poetry. Their ideas and slogans were so vague that the Symbolists were usually unable to describe in any meaningful way the dynamics of their own poetry; [13] and the problem is complicated by the fact that early critical works (based on these vague slogans) were as much responsible as the poetry itself for the rise of Symbolism in Europe and America. Since Arthur Symons, one of the great early proselytizers of Symbolism in the English-speaking world, got lost in transmitting the theories of Mallarmé or Rimbaud, the relation of his

co-Symbolists, and (b) that neither the praise nor the practice of "the aesthetic unity of created art" is limited to the poets in question; only the persistent use of the word *symbol* is new, and its use, then as now, is rather vague. See Northrop Frye, "Three Meanings of Symbolism," *Yale French Studies,* and W. K. Wimsatt, "Two Meanings of Symbolism," reprinted in his *Hateful Contraries,* pp. 51-71.

12. See E. Engelberg, *The Symbolist Poem,* p. 22, as well as the Frye and Wimsatt essays cited in n. 11.

13. As some of the citations in notes 5-8 may illustrate. Moréas's concept of *la bonne langue* in his *Manifeste Littéraire* is another example. Early Symbolists' statements have a free-swinging or evangelical quality which often makes for inaccurate or overly general views of their own poetics; e.g. Stuart Merrill's "Credo" in his *Prose et Vers.*

"English Symbolists" to the original French ones becomes questionable. Later criticism has compounded the problem by substituting for the long-suffering term *symbol* [14] such concepts as *image,* [15] *metaphor,* [16] and *literary monad.* [17]

Thus it is clear that Symbolism is not a relatively unified set of views that may be put forth in a manifesto (although this was attempted on several occasions), but a collection of independent and often poorly delineated attitudes. Considered in its larger context of time and geography, Symbolism becomes a most awkward concept to work with. Furthermore, the "Symbolist aesthetic" often fails as a description of the dynamics of Symbolist poetry, ending up as a catalogue of nonexclusive goals. From the standpoint of literary aesthetics at any rate, one is forced to agree with Lehmann that the "terms 'literary symbol' and 'symbolist' are terms which . . . should never have been allowed to remain in usage." [18]

Who Were the Real Symbolists?

The final difficulty (raised in part by the historical and doctrinal problems already outlined) is the problem of distinguishing, even within historical and national boundaries, the "true" Symbolists from their non-Symbolist contemporaries. Clearly, there are two alternative approaches to this problem: we can accept as "Symbolists" only those poets who called themselves by that name, or we can attempt to establish some independent critical criterion and

14. Some later critics have respected this usage. While they constitute a majority, the word is often used with some reservations or qualification. See Frye, "Three Meanings of Symbolism."

15. E.g. Sv. Johansen, *Le Symbolisme.*

16. D. A. K. Aish, *La Métaphore dans l'œuvre de S. Mallarmé,* is an example. Cf. Paul Claudel's statement that "la metaphore, l'iambe fondamental . . . est l'art autochtone employé par tout ce qui naît," *Art poétique,* p. 51.

17. This is Lehmann's proposed substitute for *symbol* (*Symbolist Aesthetic,* p. 315).

18. Ibid., p. 316.

create a distinction on that basis alone. In other words, *Symbolist* can be used as a purely conventional term, or it can be accepted as a meaningful critical definition which is (or should be) necessarily devoid of purely conventional significance.

The first alternative would obviously exclude poets like Verlaine (who consistently rejected the epithet *Symbolist*), Rimbaud (who had stopped writing before he ever heard of Symbolism), and perhaps even Mallarmé (quoted as saying, "J'abomine les écoles . . . je suis un solitaire"),[19] while admitting indiscriminately all of their contemporaries who, for one reason or another, chose to associate publicly with the Symbolist school. But the second alternative is equally problematical, given the great diversity of beliefs about poetry among its various practitioners and their disagreement as to the meaning of key critical concepts (such as *symbol*); and this confusion makes it impossible to group any sizeable number of poets under one critical standard or set of standards.

The traditional solution to this problem has been a compromise between the above alternatives. *Symbolism* has been ostensively defined by means of a list of some of the broad aims of the *école symboliste* ("evocativeness," "musicality," etc.) and a roster of Symbolist poets (based in part on the poets' own claims and disclaimers, and in part on later critical evaluations). Thus, in spite of the fact that there are few characteristics in the poetry of W. B. Yeats that are reminiscent of Mallarmé or Rimbaud,[20] we tend today to think of Yeats as a Symbolist poet, largely because of the famous historical confusion of Symbolism with symbolism,[21]

19. Quoted in C. A. Hackett, *Modern French Poetry (from Baudelaire to the Present Day)*, p. xi.

20. Only in his last years did Yeats show a stylistic resemblance to the Symbolists, and even that is far from strong; most of his verse might be better compared to that of the Parnassians or Verlaine.

21. That is, the use of symbols vs. the literary movement. For a discussion of this question in regard to Yeats and others, see Engelberg, *Symbolist Poem*, pp. 22-28.

reinforced by his own essays on Symbolism, by his visit to the Paris literary *cénacles* in 1894, and by Arthur Symons's reference to him as "the chief representative of that movement in our country." [22] At the same time, Oscar Wilde is usually excluded from the Symbolists, despite his association with Mallarmé (whom he addressed as "Cher Maître") and his early activity in the movement.[23] Among the American poets, Pound, Eliot, Stevens, and Hart Crane are "in the Symbolist tradition," [24] but we do not speak of an American Symbolist movement. In other words, we have been neither wholly critical nor wholly conventional in our use of the term *Symbolist*.

In trying to define Symbolism—whether historically, in regard to its doctrine, or simply to its membership—one is ultimately led to the conclusion that it differs in kind from most of the other "isms" in literature. Its appearance did not, for example, herald the massive shift in sensibilities that Romanticism did, nor did Symbolism bring to literature the kind of aesthetic program characteristic of Surrealism, Naturalism, and so forth. Rather, the term *Symbolism* today refers to a movement of unclear chronology and of aesthetic goals so vague and inconsistent as to be meaningless—a movement whose membership is defined by a patchwork of arbitrary convention and random applications of some critical standard. In fact, this movement might not have considered itself as such at all were it not for a peculiar aware-

22. Arthur Symons, *The Symbolist Movement in Literature*, p. xix.
23. Especially by the Russians; cf. the early Russian study of Symbolism by Ellis' (Kobylinskij), *Russkie Simvolisty*, p. 3 and passim.
24. For full discussions of Pound, Eliot, and Stevens, and their Symbolist heritage, see R. Taupin, *l'Influence du symbolisme français sur la poésie américaine*. Crane has been so considered, partly because of his own statements in his letters (see also the Rimbaud epigraph to *White Buildings*, Crane's first book), as well as an early fondness for Jules Laforgue; see Warren Ramsey, "Crane and Laforgue," in *Jules Laforgue and the Ironic Inheritance*, pp. 213-22.

ness of literary history on the part of the Symbolists and their critics; as will be seen, they were the "Symbolists" partly because they were so conscious of the previous existence of "Classicists" and "Romanticists." In any case, were it not for a singular poetic quality introduced by the Symbolists, one might certainly be justified in dismissing the term *Symbolist* entirely, or relegating the "Symbolist schools" in various literatures to the level of such fleeting phenomena as Romanism, Letterism, or Imagism.

This trait—that strangeness discussed in regard to Maeterlinck and Dylan—is, as I have already suggested, most important in two ways: as the one element that comes close to unifying the "Symbolists" in various literatures and setting them off from their predecessors, and as the source of a long-term influence that Symbolism had on the course of literary history, the factor that makes the Symbolist movement as such worthy of sustained consideration. For these reasons, the proper definition of Symbolism must ultimately focus on *strangeness,* and in this it will differ from the kinds of definitions of literary movements normally found. In other words, the Symbolist movement must be discussed primarily in terms of its style, for the *way they wrote* defines the Symbolists as a group more directly than their oft-emphasized mystical sensibilities,[25] the debate over "la poésie pure," or any of the Symbolists' other notorieties.

If this poetic strangeness emerges as Symbolism's prime characteristic, however, then there is a problem with the historical survey set forth in this chapter, which does not account for its origin. In other words, considering the fact that this taste for mysteriousness reappears in various forms throughout Symbolist poetry—in a sonnet by Mallarmé or Saint-Pol-Roux, in an enigmatic lyric by Rimbaud or Blok —then what we need is a literary history of the time that can indicate its source.

25. This is the characteristic emphasized in C. M. Bowra, *The Heritage of Symbolism,* pp. 1-16.

2. History and Strangeness

Europe in the late nineteenth century was a place of tension in the realm of ideas and literature. It was not unlike America in the present day: the public eye was fixed on the scientific and technological advances of the times, which produced new, seemingly limitless tools for man's attempt to embrace the whole of his existence. And yet there was also a growing apprehension about the future of human values in the new world: many people felt that some sort of turning point would soon be reached and were concerned about the new direction to be taken. There was much activity in the arts. Just as the general public today is hostile to electronic music and experimental films, so the nineteenth century ridiculed and scorned the then "far-out" movements in painting and in poetry.

The bohemians of the day wandered in and out of a number of literary cliques, called—as we have seen—by various names, but most often "the Decadents" and later "the Symbolists." The former was an insult—one that some artists welcomed—from bourgeois society. When, at Moréas's urging, the latter name gained currency, most people viewed the word *Symbolist* as a polite substitution for *Decadent*.

Whether Decadents or Symbolists, one thing is clear about these writers: they were at odds with the prevailing current of the times, particularly with the ideas that were being written and talked about in the fashionable weeklies and in books brought out by the leading publishing houses of the day. In short, the Symbolists were, as we would put it these days, "culturally alienated." In seeking to fix on the source of their grievances, they sifted through various components of their modern world and, as writers, often ended up challenging current theories about art. For the Symbolists in France this meant a certain hostility to the Positivist current in French philosophy.[1] The Russian Symbolists had a

1. Lehmann, in *Symbolist Aesthetic,* strongly emphasizes the Sym-

similar if more immediate source of irritation: the school of "social literary criticism," which had grown out of the writings of V. G. Belinskij, N. A. Dobroljubov, N. G. Černyševskij, and D. L. Pisarev. These critics, writing in the middle of the nineteenth century, had stressed the unavoidable social orientation of literature, an orientation that leads to (a) a diminution of the importance of the individual in literature, either as a subject of consideration or as the poet himself;[2] (b) emphasis on the concept of a national literature, resulting from the influence of certain established national characteristics on a country's writers;[3] and (c) the necessary equation of poetry with perceivable reality. Similarities between these literary critics and the French Positivists may be seen, but the Russian critics were much more emphatic in such matters as the role of the fantastic in literature:

> The raging of a sleeping man or the dreams of a madman are the invention of fantasy; they are not, however, poetry. The inventions of poetry must have some set characteristic which distinguishes them from inventions of all other kind. *Poetry is the creative reproduction of reality as possibility.* Therefore, that which cannot be in reality would be equally false in poetry: in other words, that which cannot exist in reality cannot be poetic. . . .

---

bolists' anti-Positivism (pp. 21-34). One must, however, be wary of overstating the case, inasmuch as some of the Symbolists' own views on "literary evolution" (cited later in this chapter) derive much from the Positivists. Cf. René Wellek's discussion of Positivism and social criticism in vols. 3 and 4 of his *A History of Modern Criticism.*

2. See R. E. Matlaw, *Belinsky, Chernyshevsky and Dobroliubov,* pp. 118-19 and 140 ff.

3. Thus Belinskij: "Every nation, according to its character . . . contributes its share to mankind's common treasure of achievements. . . . Literature must necessarily be the expression, the symbol of a nation's inner life" (trans. in V. G. Belinsky, *Selected Philosophical Works,* pp. 12-14).

To be a poet, one must not express petty desires, nor the dreaming of idle fantasy, nor the recording of feeling, nor modish sorrow, but a deep sympathy with the issues of reality of one's own time.[4]

The current of resentment that grew up around such doctrines became part of the intellectual background of the late nineteenth century in Russia. It expressed itself most directly in the attacks of A. L. Volynskij (Akim Flekser) on Belinksij and the social critics.[5]

Simultaneous to the Symbolists' reaction to social criticism was a growing feeling of resentment toward scientific accomplishments and the new technology. This was particularly true for the French Symbolists. Their antipathy to scientific advances expressed itself either in a feigned ignorance of the nineteenth century (as in the *école romane* poets, who usually wrote about pre-nineteenth-century subjects), or, more actively, in mock borrowings from scientific lingo; for science had imposed strange new formulas on the language:

Puis elle chante. O
Si gai, si facile,
Et visible à l'œil nu...
—Je chante avec elle,—[6]

Femme, ôte-toi de là, et va t'accroupir dans un
coin; tes yeux m'attendrissent, et tu ferais mieux
de refermer le conduit de tes glandes lacrymales.[7]

More of a threat than scientific language was the very notion that science had an unsurpassable method of apprehending the world, and that everything poetry had touched would

4. V. G. Belinskij, *O Klassikax Russkoj Literatury*, p. 305.
5. See Poggioli, *Poets of Russia*, pp. 55-56, and M. Slonim, *Modern Russian Literature*, p. 86.
6. From Rimbaud's "Age d'Or" (*Œuvres*, p. 162).
7. Le Comte de Lautréamont (Isidore Ducasse), *Les Chants de Maldoror*, reprinted in his *Œuvres complètes*, p. 326.

sooner or later have to submit to scientific ordering. The sea, so long a symbol of the infinite and the unknowable, was now subject to scientific investigation like everything else; and for the young poets, the Symbolists, it became all the more menacing and hostile, a kind of "last hold-out" of the natural world against the onrush of scientific accomplishments: [8]

> Vieil océan, les hommes, malgré l'excellence de leurs méthodes, ne sont pas encore parvenus, aidés par les moyens d'investigations de la science, à mesurer la profondeur vertigineuse de tes abîmes. . . . Vieil océan, tu es si puissant, que les hommes l'ont appris à leurs propres dépens. Ils ont beau employer toutes les ressources de leur génie—incapables de te dominer.[9]

Et, peut-être, les mâts, invitant les orages
Sont-ils de ceux qu'un vent penche sur les naufrages
Perdus sans mâts, sans mâts, ni fertiles îlots. . .
Mais, ô mon cœur, entends le chant des matelots! [10]

Même certains de vous, les plus hardiment braves
Charrient encor le sang des aieux scandinaves. . .
Qui partaient vers la mort sur leurs vaisseaux en flammes,
Sans focs, sans matelots, sans boussole, sans rames,

8. Accomplishments is an important word here, for it was not the systematic aspect of scientific investigation that caused the uneasiness. Indeed, method and system are often the subject of great praise on the part of the Symbolists. See Lautréamont's litany in *Maldoror*, beginning "O mathématiques sévères" (*Œuvres complètes*, p. 132), Paul Valéry's essay, "Introduction à la méthode de Leonard de Vinci" (first printed in the *Nouvelle Revue*, August 1895), and Rimbaud's fascination with alchemical systems (e.g. the "Alchimie du Verbe" section of *Une Saison en enfer*, reprinted in his *Œuvres complètes*, p. 228). The fascination with method goes back to Baudelaire's admiration of Poe's "Philosophy of Composition" and ratiocination.

9. Lautréamont, pp. 57-59.

10. From Mallarmé's "Brise marine," in his *Œuvres complètes*, p. 38.

Et se couchaient, à l'heure où le soir est vermeil,
Ivres, dans un tombeau de flots et de soleil.[11]

The self-destructive aspect of the above passages is not exclusively "Symbolist," it is characteristic of any literature at odds with its own time. But how desperate the Symbolists' estrangement must have been, to cause them to find solace in the thought of destruction-despite-technology—to cry out, with Valerij Brjusov, for a new race of Huns to overrun Western civilization! [12]

Out of a sense of cultural alienation grew the feeling of individual isolation and the glorification of one's own singleness. In this the Symbolists regarded some of the speculative thinkers of nineteenth-century Germany as close spiritual allies. For example, in his eulogy of his friend, Villiers de l'Isle-Adam, Mallarmé praises him for bringing Hegel to the *école symboliste,* for him, a very important event. Moreover, the individualism of Fichte and Schopenhauer, carried over into aesthetics in the distinction made between art and all other forms of human activity, is an obvious area of agreement between the French Symbolists and the German philosophers.[13]

The extent to which these philosophers appealed to the early Symbolists may best be seen in the superhuman figure who is the focal point of so many Symbolist novels, plays, and stories. Des Esseintes (a character of Huysmans), Axël (Villiers de l'Isle-Adam), the speaker of Rimbaud's *Illuminations* and *Une Saison en Enfer,* Maldoror (Lautréa-

11. From E. Verhaeren's "Les Plages," in his *"Choix de Poèmes* p. 136.
12. Brjusov's poem, "Grjaduščie Gunny" [the Coming Huns] is reprinted and discussed in Chapter 4 of the present study.
13. "Par rapport à l'homme, sujet pensant, le monde, tout ce qui est extérieur au moi, n'éxiste que selon l'idée qu'il s'en fait . . . C'est ce que Schopenhauer a vulgarisé sous cette formule si simple et si claire, 'Le monde est ma représentation' " (R. de Gourmont, Préface, *Le Livre des masques*).

mont), Igitur (Mallarmé), M. Teste (Valéry)—all are heroes possessed of a single-minded search into their own beings. They live on the outskirts of society, and their views are continually counterpointed to those of "la foule"; to this extent, their archetype, is another hero of Villiers de l'Isle-Adam, the blind beggar who, above the din of the crowd's successive "Vive l'Empereur," "Vive la Républ-ique," or "Vive la Commune," chants his lonely alexan-drine, "Prenez pitié d'un pauvre aveugle, s'il vous plaît." [14] And, like the beggar, the Symbolist heroes can only laugh at those caught up in the relativity implicit in mundane existence. Society's values are continually mocked; and even love, for the Symbolist hero, is transformed into rape, perversion, and death.[15] His search, contemporary to Nietzsche's, inevitably leads him *jenseits von Gut und Böse.*

The relationship of the Russian Symbolists to the German idealistic philosophers was even more intense. The influence of Kant, Hegel, and Schopenhauer was still felt, but be-cause Russian Symbolism came slightly later, Nietzsche's im-pact was stronger.[16] Also, Russian Symbolism coincided historically with a religious and philosophical revival inside Russia (its unorthodoxy is well represented in Rozanov and Šestov),[17] and the historical interweaving of these three strands—literary, religious, and philosophical—is sym-bolized in the work of Vladimir Solovĕv. His importance— in attacking the "dead-end" of Positivist philosophy and

14. In his story "Vox populi," in *Contes cruels,* p. 63.

15. An exception here is Valéry's happily married M. Teste.

16. See Poggioli, *Poets of Russia,* pp. 62, 119; Slonim, *Modern Russian Literature,* pp. 103-04. Ellis's (Kobylinskij) early study, *Russkie Simvolisty,* devotes nearly half its general discussion to Nietzsche (pp. 24-28 and passim). Belyj, *Vospominanija ob A. Bloke* [Memoirs about Aleksandr Blok], also speaks of him in some detail (pp. 16-18 and passim).

17. For a comparison of these two Russian thinkers in regard to Russian Symbolism, see D. S. Mirsky, *Contemporary Russian Litera-ture,* pp. 163-75.

applauding the German idealists,[18] in developing his own religious mysticism and evolving a new poetry from it— cannot be too strongly emphasized.[19]

The Symbolists, then, were acutely aware of a barrier between themselves and "the others." In one sense, as we have seen, "the others" were the exponents of critical and philosophical tendencies that the Symbolists found disagreeable. But in a larger sense they were society itself, and society's history. Bolstered by a few slogans culled from Schopenhauer and his compatriots, many of the emerging poets were anxious to proclaim their independence from the whole Establishment, including its literary branch. In short, they sought to express their estrangement out loud and in their poetry.

Onto the scene stepped the new poets—Jean Moréas, Stéphane Mallarmé, and a handful of others. Some had already been associated with the last wave of Romanticism and fell in with the *Parnasse Contemporain,* a review of growing importance. Although its pages contained poems which, for the most part, lacked the shimmering mystery of later Symbolist poems, one can find in them the continuing feeling of separation, the rejection of the quotidian that we assocate with the Symbolists. Here is the theme of *l'évasion* —escape—championed by Baudelaire. "The Flesh is sad, alas!" begins Mallarmé's *Brise marine* (which first appeared in the *Parnasse*), "and I have read all the books. / Away, to get away! . . ." The magazine was a beginning for the Symbolists, and it was being read as far away as Russia.

18. Most specifically in his doctoral thesis "Crisis in Western Philosophy" (1874), subtitled "Against the Positivists." The French translation, *Crise de la philosophie occidentale,* contains an excellent introduction by M. Herman. For the influence of the German idealists on Solovёv, see F. Stepun, *Mystische Weltschau,* pp. 16 and ff.

19. Solovёv's influence is amply shown in separate chapters of Mirsky, Poggioli, and Slonim. For his particular influence on Blok, see F. D. Reeve, *Aleksandr Blok,* pp. 20-31.

Yet these early days were not without their anxieties, and the *Parnasse* was the focal point of the Symbolists' ambivalence toward Romanticism. On the one hand, some of the most current trends in "new Romantic" poetry were quite appealing: its deemphasis of lived experience in favor of the purely imaginative, its attraction to the mysterious and artificial, and—above all—its obsession with occult beauty. On the other hand, Romanticism was dead, and among the young poets was a pervasive sense that the time had come for a new movement in poetry to equal Romanticism and Classicism. An awareness of literary history among the French and Russians was crucial here.[20] A new "ism" was needed, to express the separateness of the young poets and also as a vehicle for their desire for newness; and although its direction was still uncertain, the feeling of a coming change was in the air. Rimbaud sums up much of the prevailing sentiment, in the second half of his May 15 letter to Demeny, and his tone captures the general enthusiasm:

> . . . demandons aux poètes du nouveau,—idées et formes. Tous les habiles croiraient bientôt avoir satisfait à cette demande.—Ce n'est pas cela:
>
> Les premiers romantiques ont été voyants sans trop bien s'en rendre compte: la culture de leurs âmes s'est commencée aux accidents . . .

20. It would be difficult to demonstrate that the lack of Symbolist *movement* in England is due to a lack of awareness of an English Romantic movement (or a refusal to think in such terms, which would have the same effect), but I must admit to being tempted by such thinking. René Wellek indicates the lack of awareness in England (R. Wellek and A. Warren, *Theory of Literature,* p. 264), and this, coupled with statements such as that of Arthur Symons in reference to Symbolism ("France is the country of movements, and it is naturally in France that I have studied the development of a principle which is spreading throughout other countries . . ."—from the dedication of his *Symbolist Movement in Literature*), may lend credence to such a proposition. For the tone of Symon's statement (despite earlier references to "our country" and "the Irish literary movement")

> Les seconds romantiques sont très voyants: Th.
> Gautier, Lec. de Lille, Th. de Banville. Mais inspecter
> l'invisible et entendre l'inouï étant autre chose que
> reprendre l'esprit des choses mortes, Baudelaire est le
> premier voyant, roi des poètes, un vrai dieu! Encore
> a-t-il vécu dans un milieu trop artiste; et la forme si
> vantée en lui est mesquine: les inventions d'inconnu
> réclament des formes nouvelles.[21]

The same attitude is picked up in Gustave Kahn's preface
to his *Premiers Poèmes:*

> Ah! ceci n'est point une attaque contre les poètes du
> passé: nous déclarions récemment que le symbolisme
> était une conséquence logique et fatale du romantisme
> . . . Si l'oreille des romantiques différait de celle des
> classiques, la nôtre a d'autres besoins que les leurs. Le
> sens des couleurs change, le sens de la cadence poétique
> change aussi; insensiblement, sans doute! mais il y a
> toujours un moment où l'on s'en aperçoit, et l'évolution
> assez prolongée est devenue suffisamment nette pour
> s'appeler une transformation.

In Moréas's famous manifesto (*Figaro Littéraire,* September
18, 1886) the sense of the new era is understandably much
stronger:

> Il serait superflu de faire observer que chaque nouvelle
> phase évolutive de l'art correspond exactement à la
> décrépitude sénile, à l'inéluctable fin d'école immédiate-
> ment antérieure . . .
>
> Ainsi, le romantisme, après avoir sonné tous les
> tumultueux tocsins de la révolte, après avoir eu ses

---

is that literary movements are foreign to the British Isles; and it is
curious to note that Symons, in describing the expansion of Symbolism across the Continent, omits Wilde and his compatriots from consideration, although neither Mallarmé nor the Russians had seen fit
to do so.

21. Rimbaud, *Œuvres,* pp. 348-49.

jours de gloire et de bataille, perdit de sa force et de
sa grâce, abdiqua ses audaces héroïques, se fit rangé,
sceptique et plein de bon sens; dans l'honorable et
mesquine tentative des Parnassians, il espéra de fal-
lacieux renouveaux, puis, finalement, tel un monarque
tombé en enfance, il se laissa déposer par le naturalisme
auquel on ne peut accorder sérieusement qu'une valeur
de protestation, légitime mais avisée, contre les fadeurs
de quelques romanciers alors à la mode.

Une nouvelle manifestation d'art était donc attendue,
nécessaire, inévitable. Cette manifestation, couvée
depuis longtemps, vient d'éclore.[22]

The result of this kind of enthusiasm was the *mêlée symboliste* of the 1880s and 1890s. The many competing schools
and ideologies—Surnaturalism, Decadentism, Instrument-
ism, Symbolism, and Romanism—and the large number of
periodicals publishing important Symbolist poetry [23] show
to what extent this was a period of intense and searching
literary creation.

The sense that the Romantic era was ending and the
necessity of finding a new direction is even more evident in
Russia than in France. It may be seen in Solovëv's "Second
Coming" writings, in Merežkovskij's "Before the Dawn," in
Blok's "Dawns," [24] and in critical writings of the day.[25] By
1893, an awareness of the French Symbolists began to appear among the Russian poets: Brjusov, who had just sub-
mitted his Mallarmé translations to a publisher two weeks
earlier, wrote in his diary on March 22, 1893:

What if I should take it into my head to write a treatise
on spectral analysis in Homeric language? I wouldn't

22. Reprinted in Michaud, *La Doctrine symboliste,* pp. 24-25.
23. K. Cornell, *The Symbolist Movement,* lists in an appendix 55
of the most important Symbolist periodicals between 1881 and 1889.
24. Poggioli, *Poets of Russia,* pp. 83 and 126, respectively.
25. Thus Slonim (*Modern Russian Literature,* p. 87) cites S.
Djagilev, editor of *Mir Iskusstva,* writing of "a new climate, and of
new ideas which, like precious fragrance, fill the air."

have the words and expressions. Well then, suppose I were to express, in the language of Pushkin, the *Fin de siècle* awareness! No, I need symbolism! [26]

This is, in many respects, the strongest evidence of the kind of search that was going on: what Brjusov pinpoints is an inability of the poetic ideal (Homer, Pushkin) to deal with the concerns of the day (spectral analysis, fin-de-siècle). Symbolism was, at least at first, a way out of the poetic impasse, just as Solovëv had seen German idealism as a way out of the impasse created by Positivism in Western philosophy.[27] What happened later, of course, was a confluence of these religious, philosophical, and literary tendencies, that strengthened the end-of-an-era sentiment and made the inevitability of a new path (literary, religious, and philosophical) more evident than before.[28] Belyj describes the era in his *Recollections of A. Blok:*

> [Merežkovskij's] slogan, "Either us or no one," became the motto of some of the young people, and had something in common with the old prophecy of Agrippa Nettengeimskij and the "book of flashes" about the significance of the year 1900 as the turning point of an epoch. We joined these slogans with the fancies of Solovëv about the Third Testament, the Realm of Spirit. The cessation of old ways went down as the End of the World, and the news of the era was the Second Coming. We had a sense of the apocalyptical rhythm of time. We hastened towards the Beginning across the End.
>
> This feeling of an end, of a boundary between the consciousness of the Decadents of the 90's and the

---

26. V. Brjusov, *Dnevniki, 1891-1910,* p. 13.

27. See Solovëv, *Crise de la philosophie occidentale,* p. 25 and ff. of the Introduction. Solovëv saw the influence of Schopenhauer and Hartmann as most important in this respect.

28. Cf. V. Žirmunskij, *Voprosy Teorii Literatury,* pp. 278-81, and Reeve, *Aleksandr Blok,* pp. 1-5.

consciousness of the young Symbolists of the twentieth
century, the physiologicality, the concreteness of the
perception of the dawn, the fact of daybreak and the
inevitability of this fact, as well as the bewilderment
and difficulty in understanding the reasons for the
dawning—that is what was occupying our attention.
Many perceived the arrival of the new age not as the
evolution of an ideology, but as the actual appearance
in them of new organs of time-perception. The ideological explanations of the Symbolists, psychological,
logical, mystical, sociological and religious, bore the
character of lame chance-hypotheses. The fact of this
feeling of the dawning remained.[29]

The push toward innovation, toward something new in
literature, was so strong among the emerging poets of the
late nineteenth century that it is difficult to try to recapture
it after the fact. It is natural for each generation of poets
to want a poetry of its own age; obviously, the drive toward
innovation is almost a constant force in literary history. But
how much stronger it must have been for the Symbolists, so
keenly aware of a barrier between themselves and the
established philosophical and critical attitudes of the day
—a barrier which, in the eyes of some, separated them
from society itself. And how much stronger still the desire
to innovate must have been when—in France to a certain
extent, but most of all in Russia—the twentieth century
loomed as an apocalyptic Turning Point in the history of
mankind. These were not large, impersonal forces acting
upon the young writers; they were feelings that the Symbolists experienced themselves very strongly, feelings that
can best be seen in their own early manifestos, articles, and
other writings.

And so it was that in their search for newness the Symbolists gradually hit upon mystery—*strangeness*—as the

29. Belyj, *Vospominanija ob A. Bloke,* p. 15.

ultimate poetic effect. How this was achieved will be discussed shortly; for the present it is important to understand how such a "poetry of strangeness" related to the mood of the times. For the Symbolists, to write a poem in the new "strange" style was to say in their poetry precisely the same thing they said in expository prose when they wrote about their alienation from contemporary standards and their sense of the coming apocalypse. One strangeness corresponded to the other. That is, their own feelings of strangeness (in the senses of estrangement, alienation, individual isolation, and newness) found expression in a poetry of strangeness (in the senses of mystery, incomprehensibility, innovation).

This is no idle play on words. There is a connection between these various meanings of the word *strangeness,* and it is precisely that connection which joins what we know about Symbolist history to what we can see about Symbolist poetry. That which is mysterious is always set off, separate from us, foreign; and with mysteriousness the Symbolists created a barrier parallel to those present in their thinking about the New Age, the German philosophers, art and society. For, in the poetry of strangeness the relationship between poet and reader also contains a barrier: a Symbolist poem cannot be "what oft was thought, but ne'er so well expressed," but is, rather, something foreign, something which never wholly becomes the reader's own. To be mysterious is to express separation and disjunction; [30] but it is also to be *new,* for mystery is continuously new.

Most of all this is true of language. To be sure, we can discover many kinds of mysteriousness in Symbolist writings. One can point to their fascination with religious mys-

---

30. This is an idea basic to the human spirit and upon it are predicated most of mankind's observances and ceremonies of religious mystery, of G–d as the "wholly other" (*ganz andere*). One book devoted to exploring this connection is Mircea Eliade's *The Sacred and the Profane;* see also Rudolf Otto, *The Idea of the Holy.*

tery,[31] their taste for occultism and preoccupation with folk magic and the like,[32] their Satanism and adventures in the realm of "forbidden tastes." [33] But it is in the mysterious

31. Particularly those of the Russian Symbolists (Merežkovskij, Gippius, Brjusov, Blok's Solověv-inspired "Beautiful Lady" cycle, Vjač. Ivanov, and the later works of Belyj); but also, among the French, Huysmans, Verhaeren, Saint-Pol-Roux, Villiers de l'Isle-Adam, and Paul Claudel.

32. This is a vast subject, to which I can only allude. We find, in addition to various occultist sects—Baudelaire's Swedenborgism, Yeats's Rosicrucianism, Belyj's anthroposophy, Crane's pass with Gurdjieff—a general interest among the Symbolists in Indian religious systems and the like. The allure of folklore and folk magic was equally widespread and was not limited to literary circles. Books such as Eliphas Lévi's *Dogme et rituel de la haute magie,* while influencing several Symbolists (for its effect on Villier's *Axel,* see P. Mariel's introduction to the 1960 Paris reprint; a copy of S. L. M. Mathers's translation of the book was found in Yeats's library), enjoyed no small popularity on the open market. The same was true in England, with Madame Blavatsky and S. L. M. Mathers (see H. R. Bachchan, *W. B. Yeats and Occultism*). More directly relevant to folk beliefs and their mysteries was the new awareness of folklore which grew up with the great anthropological studies of the time— Frazer's *The Golden Bough* (1890–1915) in England, and Savčenko and, later, Propp in Russia. This new awareness was particularly evident in Ireland's Celtic Revival literature, as well as in a miniature Celtic revival that was led in France by such eminent Bretons as Anatole Le Braz and Villiers. One might also draw a parallel between these efforts and T. S. Eliot's later simultaneous interest in both the French Symbolists (notably Laforgue and Corbière) and the Grail legend.

33. Although a tradition of the aesthetic evil may be traced to before the nineteenth century (for a complete study of it, see M. Praz, *Romantic Agony*), the Symbolists perceived it as an essentially new and strange phenomenon in literature. For them the tradition began with *Les Fleurs du mal,* where the search for newness is inevitably linked with evil:

> Plonger au fond du gouffre, Enfer ou Ciel, qu'importe?
> Au fond de l'inconnu, pour trouver du nouveau!

It continues in France with Rimbaud, Lautréamont, the *Contes cruels* of Villiers, Barbey d'Aurevilly's *Diaboliques,* Laforgue, and Corbière. In Russia, the rationale was much the same: "On behalf of the New and often incomprehensible *language* of Symbolist poetry that strangeness finds its most forceful expression. For language, we humans feel, is what we have in common, it is an organic bond among living beings, a symbol of our community. When, in Symbolist poetry, language itself turns mysterious, it makes a powerful assertion—that even in language men stand apart, that the essence of things is beyond agreement. And this is the point at which the two strangenesses are united. Mystery is an assertion that a barrier exists, and our community, our having-in-common, is denied in a poem where language itself becomes mysterious and utterly strange. The Symbolists may not have been the first "alienated" movement in literature, but they were the first to identify alienation with mystery, noncommunion with noncommunication.

Beauty," wrote Merežkovskij, "we break all commandments" (see Poggioli, pp. 84-85). Among the Russian Satanists were Sologub and Brjusov.

3.   The Prince and His Star

The stylistic problem faced by the Symbolist poet was how to make a poem strange. Of course, it is unlikely that he posed the question to himself in such a conscious way: he simply wrote poems, and each poem was itself an answer. A good answer, a satisfying answer, was followed by another attempt along the same lines; a bad answer was rejected and its direction abandoned.

Poetic strangeness, as noted earlier, first took the form of strange subjects—remote times and civilizations, taboo tastes and delights, the "plaisirs artificiels" praised by the master Baudelaire. There were also strange verse forms, which destroyed the sacred alexandrine line (again following Baudelaire) and introduced new, short, sing-song lyrics, "refrains niais, rythmes naïfs." [1] And then there was something else, more diffuse and all-encompassing, a revolutionary technique—perhaps a whole new way of writing. It was the use of "symbols," Moréas and the others said; but as has been shown (Chapter 1), this did not go very far in describing it.

Surely this style of writing went further than Baudelaire, further than anything else that had been done, and the new poetry shimmered with a beauty unknown before—but what was it exactly, this use of "symbols"? Again, the poet is interested in writing poems, not literary criticism; if he can keep creating this new effect without having to explain it satisfactorily, he will. And, as has been seen from the morass that is the Symbolists' terminology, this is precisely what

1. The phrase is from Rimbaud's "Une Saison en Enfer" (*Œuvres*, p. 228). Gustave Kahn, Jules Laforgue, and Tristan Corbière were the most influential in regard to verse-form innovations. Kahn, claiming to have invented *vers libre*, divided his colleagues into two other groups: those who, like Mallarmé sought to "essentialize" poetry in its already existing forms, and those who, like Verlaine, Rimbaud, and Corbière, wrote lines that were "délicieusement faux exprès" (G. Kahn, préface to, *Premiers Poèmes*, pp. 14-17); the latter group did much with off-rhyme as well.

Moréas, Mallarmé, Rimbaud, Maeterlinck, and the others did do.

The first poem to achieve this *symboliste* effect in the French language was not, however, written by any of these men. It came far earlier, preceding by four years the publication of Baudelaire's *Les Fleurs du Mal*—in other words, it came long before the word *Symbolist* was coined. "El Desdichado" by Gérard de Nerval is still something of a wild, flashing poem today; it is difficult to imagine how this archetypal Symbolist piece must have looked to the casual reader of *Le Mousquetaire* as he opened his issue of December 10, 1853:

El Desdichado

Je suis le ténébreux—le veuf—l'inconsolé,
Le prince d'Aquitaine à la tour abolie:
Ma seule *étoile* est morte,—et mon luth constellé
Porte le *soleil* noir de la *Mélancolie*.

Dans la nuit du tombeau, toi qui m'as consolé,
Rends-moi le Pausilippe et la mer d'Italie,
La fleur qui plaisait tant à mon coeur désolé
Et la treille où le pampre à la rose s'allie.

Suis-je Amour ou Phébus? . . . Lusignan ou Biron?
Mon front est rouge encor du baiser de la reine;
J'ai rêvé dans la grotte où nage la sirène . . .

Et j'ai deux fois vainqueur traversé l'Achéron:
Modulant tour à tour sur la lyre d'Orphée
Les soupirs de la sainte et les cris de la fée.[2]

A first reading of the sonnet will leave the reader, at the very least, puzzled. If "El Desdichado" is as good a poem as I feel it to be, that same first reading—or subsequent readings—may catch the reader up in some of the mystery of the lonely speaker's plight: the allusions to his fabulous adventures in a world of queens, castles, and dreamy sea-caves

2. G. de Nerval, *Œuvres, 1* : 693-95.

and, for all that, his overwhelming, unconsolable sadness. But whatever else the reader may feel when he finishes it, he must at least have a sense of being "out of it," cut off from the poem—for what, after all, does he know about it?

The poem appears to be a desperate, death-bound lament of . . . El Desdichado.[3] The reader does not know who the speaker is, although apparently a good deal of the sonnet is devoted to that subject. The speaker identifies himself as the Prince of Aquitania, Cupid, Phoebus (Apollo), Lusignan, Biron—in other words, none of these, for the very profusion of names prevents the reader from taking any one of them seriously: they are metaphors, allusive comparisons. The reader knows, or senses, that this central figure is mourning some sort of loss (he is "widowed," he tells us in line 1, and unconsoled; his "star" is dead—line 3). But what has he lost—his woman? Is she dead, or simply gone?

And then, what is the meaning of these other phrases: "My brow is still red from the kiss of the queen"—which queen?—"In the night of the tomb," "I have dreamt in the grotto where the siren swims"? How does all this fit together?

My purpose in posing these questions is not to introduce a thorough gloss of the source of each mysterious fragment in the poem,[4] but to focus only on two phrases that occur early in the poem—"le prince d'Aquitaine à la tour abolie" and "ma seule étoile est morte"—and to ask, not what they mean, but how they are "strange," how they work in the poem.

"Le prince d'Aquitaine" appears to be a reference to some figure out of French history or folklore. It, and phrases

3. The title is probably not understood by most readers—it means "the disinherited"—and is the first of many uncomprehended things in the poem. It thus serves a definite function, that of distancing the reader, and furthermore anticipates the role of "Aquitaine" in placing the speaker near the Spanish border.

4. Such information is available (e.g. Lemaître's notes in Nerval, Œuvres) but, as will be seen, a knowledge of it only undercuts the poem's strangeness and undermines its overall effect.

such as "la nuit du tombeau," "le baiser de la reine," and
others, are allusions which pass unrecognized by the reader.
In each case, the implication is that some specific person or
thing or event is being referred to, but the reader does not
know who or what. He is in the same position as someone
who has never studied the *Aeneid* or heard of Dido and who,
in the course of reading Shakespeare's *Merchant of Venice,*
comes across the lines:

> In such a night
> Stood Dido with a willow in her hand
> Upon the wild sea-banks, and waft her love
> To come again to Carthage.
>   [5.1.11–14]

Not knowing who Dido is, he might still be able to piece together some of the elements of the allusion—a woman,
probably sad, bidding good-bye to her lover—but he would
definitely feel "outside" of the allusion, like a walker over-
hearing snatches of a conversation five or ten paces ahead
of him.

This is how the reader of "El Desdichado" feels, faced
with these "allusions to nowhere." "Le Prince d'Aquitaine à
la tour abolie" sounds like an allusion to some famous legendary episode in French history—but one which, strangely,
the reader doesn't quite recall. When he tries to piece together the available evidence, he receives only fragmentary
impressions: "prince" to him does not mean a specific person, but only connotes youth, royalty, and days of yore.
Likewise "Aquitaine" means "Old France," "olden days,"
perhaps also "Spain" (it is near the Spanish border), thus
reenforcing the impression created by the Spanish title. "À
la tour abolie" makes the reader think of a ruined castle,
hence also of antiquity, and suggests loneliness and "living
on borrowed time" (abolie). There is no meaningful way to
put it all together, nothing that would make a reader say
"Oh, I see!" but there is not total lack of communication

either. Like the eavesdropper, the reader has caught snatches
of a conversation and, he tells himself, perhaps it will become clear later on.

In a similar way, mystery hovers around the phrase "ma
seule étoile est morte." Taken literally it is an unlikely statement. People do not usually refer to heavenly bodies as
"mine" or "yours," and furthermore it is only modern as-
tronomers who say that stars "die" or are "born," so to say
"my only star is dead" is on two counts unacceptable in its
literal meaning. We therefore assume the phrase implies that
some "figurative" meaning is called for—but one which is
not clear.

Now *étoile* in French, like *star* in English, is one of those
words around which a whole iconography has grown up. Because it was once believed that the stars controlled the des-
tinies of men, *star* in many languages has the (now figurative)
meaning of fate or destiny. Through a similar but apparently
unrelated process, *star* also acquired the meaning "hope."
Via the Latin feminine *stella* in Roman and, later, in Christian symbolism, it gained the further significance of "beauty"
or "beautiful woman." In short, *star* is one of those words
commonly characterized as having a great many "figurative"
meanings.

One fact about such meanings is immediately apparent:
they are purely conventional. A star (the heavenly body)
has no more to do with hope, beauty, or fate than—say—
the moon, but the latter's verbal iconography has evolved
instead to inconstancy, madness, jealousy—again, for purely
conventional reasons. It is the same literary tradition that
makes lions courageous or mighty, roses beautiful, hearts the
seat of the emotions, etc. Ultimately, iconographic meanings
have a real source—an ancient belief or custom, a well-
known folk-tale or saying, in short, some piece of the civilization's *lore*—but the source is unimportant, for the lore-based
meaning has long since come into its own: it is almost part
of the language.

But not quite. For just as these meanings depend on pure

literary convention, so they come with the label "figurative" attached to them, they are not quite on a par with other meanings. When someone says, "Only the stars will decide the outcome of the game" or "Barbara is a rose," a listener will understand, as part of the meaning, that the speaker is being somewhat literary, and is "speaking figuratively." Now this "figurativeness" has nothing to do with the thing-associatedness of the usages. Were the sentences changed to read "All the stars will be in today's game" and "Barbara is a peach" the usages would no longer be perceived as "figurative"—these meanings are *too* common, they truly have been absorbed by the language.

All of this is a long way to explaining the reader's reaction to phrases like "Ma seule étoile est morte," "le soleil noir de la Mélancolie," la fleur qui plaisait tant . . ." etc. In each case the reader is aware that "star," "sun," or "flower" is rife with iconographic possibilities, and that one figurative meaning or another is being called for—but which precise meaning is unclear. The reader is not sure he has understood. If, for example, he reads on in the poem looking for some confirmation of one reading of *étoile* over the others, he is disappointed: he may suspect this "star" to mean a beautiful woman, a last hope in the speaker's life, the speaker's fate—or some combination of the three. But whichever it is, no more precise information is offered. The thing the speaker has lost only goes on to be called or associated with: "le Pausilippe," "la mer d'Italie," "la fleur qui plaisait tant à mon coeur désolé" "la treille où le pampre à la rose s'allie." These offer little help.

Now there is a basic similarity between the reader's reaction to "le prince d'Aquitaine" and "ma seule étoile est morte." In both cases, he feels there is an essential bit of information which he does not have and which is necessary to full comprehension. In the first case, it is the identity of the prince, that apparent historical or legendary figure whom the reader has somehow not heard of; in the second it is that particular "figurative" meaning of *étoile* which will make all the vague phrases after it come clear. Of course, readers don't puzzle for hours over each phrase as it appears. In "El Desdichado," the reader is grasping bits and pieces—he can surmise the speaker is lamenting the loss of someone or something, and that the speaker is that shadowy, noble, dashing figure from somewhere near the Pyrenees—and so he reads on. But the poem, for him, has a certain aura of mystery about it, due to the "missing information" which, it is implied, is necessary for full comprehension. In other words, the poet creates the strangeness by *not telling everything*, or, more precisely, by implying that not everything has been told.

This is the genius of Nerval's poem, and the fundamental discovery of the Symbolist poets. They were the first to seek out systematically this effect of withheld information, recognizing in mystery a source of beauty and depth not known in poetry before. There is a compelling urgency about Nerval's new way of writing. An anonymous communication drops onto the page, a blur: prince, tower, sadness, death, Italy, flower. Read it again. The flashing scenes group about a single idea, repeated and restated throughout the poem: the grief of deprivation or separation. Who the speaker is, what he has lost—it is important that we *not* know these things, for their haziness is what gives the sonnet its force and urgency. The point of the poem is not that we find these things out. The point of the poem is that we read it again and again, that we read it until the simple message—*veuf, inconsolé, Mélancolie*—is enough for us to glide on, until we can get so much into the poem that we can accept all its words and love their mystery.

Now I have described "le prince d'Aquitaine à la tour abolie" as an apparent allusion; the same description will fit "ma seule étoile est morte." For what we tend to call an allusion in literature is simply a reference to somebody or something outside of the immediate context but (it is assumed) within the knowledge or experience of most readers.

It may be a real person or a character from literature, a historical event or a scene from a novel, a legend, a primitive
belief, a fact of natural science, a well-known landmark—in
short, something that figures in the general lore. As has been
seen, this same stock of lore is the locus of the sought-after
meaning of *étoile*. So if an allusion can be seen as a reference to lore, it is clear that *le prince d'Aquitaine* differs from
étoile only in its specificity; the two partake of essentially the
same process.

For every allusion there is a triggering mechanism: incomplete comprehension. What makes the reader perceive
"prince d'Aquitaine" as an allusion is that, as a factual statement of the speaker's identity, it adds nothing, it is unrecognized and makes no particular sense in the poem. On the
most immediate level, he finds nothing to complete his understanding and so must go looking for some lore to help.
Similarly, what makes the reader seek a "figurative" meaning for *étoile* is the fact that, taken as "heavenly body," it
doesn't make sense: it is (like *soleil noir* later on in the
poem) a contradiction in terms, and so demands some resolution. The reader sets out to look for it.

What normally happens in an allusion is that the sought-
after lore is found and the incomprehension removed. Consider, for example, a stanza of A. E. Housman's "To an
Athlete Dying Young":

> Smart lad to slip betimes away
> From fields where glory does not stay,
> And early though the laurel grows
> It withers quicker than the rose.

Taken as botanical entities, *laurel* and *rose* don't make much
sense in the poem ("Why's he talking about flowers all of a
sudden?" the reader may ask). Incomplete comprehension
leads the reader away from these "literal" meanings to two
lore-based "figurative" meanings: for rose, feminine beauty,
and for laurel, accolade (here, as is clear from the context,
the recognition given to young athletes). With the proper

lore, the sense becomes clear: "You were smart to die at a young age, since athletic prowess fades even faster than a woman's beauty." The allusive process has been completed.

Now the precise stylistic characteristic of "El Desdichado" is that the allusive process is not satisfied but continually frustrated. Again and again the reader is confronted with what looks like an allusion (in the broad sense I have been using the term) but he is unable to find the suitable bit of iconography that will unlock the mystery. And so, as has been seen, phrases break down into their constituent parts (le prince d'Aquitaine "means" only the sum of individual associations hovering about "prince," "Aquitaine," "tour," etc.); the whole becomes disjointed and chaotic. From the shimmering fragments there emerges a pattern—the lament for something irretrievably lost—but it is like a small cry in a howling wind.

Having focused on the source of mysteriousness in the poem, it is equally important to identify two unifying elements: our knowledge of the present state of the speaker, and his attitude in his lament. Whoever he may be, emphatic restatements throughout the poem of the fact that he is *le veuf* and *l'inconsolé* continually provide a framework in which to order all the flashing allusions. For all that he is and all that he has done, he remains bereft and unconsoled. "J'ai rêvé dans la grotte où nage la sirène" is a perfect expression of his state, his fabulous experience, and his total immersion in self. The reader's awareness of this state (which begins with the first line of the poem) allows him to order all the other allusions of the poem as reiterations and elaborations of the speaker's identity. Similarly, the attitude of the speaker in the poem is clearly established. He is in a state of desperate introspection (apparent in the two parallel sets of self-characterizations beginning "Je suis" and "Suis-je"), and the magnitude of his despair is clear in the hyperboles of the second quatrain ("Rends-moi le Pausilippe . . ." etc.).

These two elements—the *persona,* or identity of the speaker of the poem, and the *tone,* the speaker's attitude toward the subject of the poem and toward the reader—constitute the "fixed star" of the poem.[5] The mystery of the speaker's grief, along with the poem's other unknowns, is softened just enough by the one thing the reader knows for certain: the speaker is "widowed" and desperate. He who has been consoled is unconsolable, the star that is dead is dead forever. The speaker's yearnings for reunion (symbolized as "the trellis where the vine to the rose is joined"— line 8) and remembrances of his own past, which together make up the rest of the poem, only throw his present state into greater relief.

"El Desdichado" was a freak occurrence—Nerval never wrote anything quite like it again, nor did anyone else for the next twenty years. But despite its early date, it cannot be called a "precursor," but must be considered the first Symbolist poem in French. The frustrated allusion, the well-defined persona and tone—these are the elements on which most of the greatest Symbolist poems are built. In its total effect, "El Desdichado" has that haziness, that strangeness, which the Symbolists valued so highly. Mallarmé spoke for all the Symbolists when he repeatedly asserted this mysteriousness—with all its mystical overtones—as poetry's central concern:

> La poésie est l'expression, par le langage humain ramené à son rythme essentiel, du sens mystérieux des aspects de l'existence, et constitue la seule tache spirituelle.[6]

> Toute chose sacrée et qui veut demeurer sacrée s'enveloppe de mystère.[7]

5. The two are hard to distinguish here, since the speaker's own identity and present melancholy are precisely the subject of the poem. A good discussion of tone and persona and the relationship between the two may be found in R. A. Brower, *Fields of Light*, pp. 19-30.
6. Mallarmé, "Definition de la poesie," in *La Vogue,* April 18, 1886 (quoted in Michaud, p. 15).
7. From Jules Huret's "Enquête Littéraire," reprinted in Mallarmé's *Œuvres Complètes.*

91762

Il doit y avoir énigme en poésie, c'est le but de la littérature.[8]

Why such a poetry of mysteriousness came to be called *symbolism* will never be entirely clear. Much of it was the work of accident, that whim (it does not seem to have been much more) that Moréas had in calling his salon group the "symboliques," a name that somehow stuck, like Impressionism.[9] But if "symbol" did have any real meaning in the minds of the Symbolists or their critics, it seems to have been, not as the name of a single trope or figure, but as a general term for the allusive phrases or images that filled their poems, "le prince d'Aquitaine," "ma seule étoile" and hundreds more, which became the inscrutable icons in their Temple of the Word. For this reason Nerval's "frustrated allusion" is of particular importance. It is the archetypal Symbolist device, as much a "symbol" as is any discrete element to be found in the Symbolists' poetry.

8. Quoted in Michaud, p. 17; cf. Mallarmé's essay "Le Mystère dans les lettres," *Œuvres Complètes,* pp. 382-87.
9. Impressionism derived its name from a critic's jeer at an early Monet painting entitled "Impression—soleil levant."

4. A Symbolist Anthology

One may find scattered examples of "frustrated allusions" as far back as the "mad songs" of Shakespeare or Jonson,[1] or in so-called nonsense verse, but the Symbolists were the first to use the device systematically and in large numbers. This technique underwent a rapid development. They tried to determine its limits, to see how far it could be extended before banishing a poem to meaninglessness. They sought new ways of incorporating the allusive technique into the poem's construction, and they also looked for other means of implying withheld information. As an illustration of this evolution, the poems that follow are presented, not in historical or national order, but developmentally—starting with poems structurally similar to "El Desdichado" and gradually moving to other forms and techniques. Although most of the poets discussed come from the French and Russian schools, a few English and American poets such as Eliot and Stevens have been mentioned, inasmuch as their debt to the French Symbolists is clearly established.[2]

Strings of Allusions

As I have shown, Nerval's incomplete allusions appear in several different forms, which might be grouped into three broad categories:

1. It is noteworthy that the "neo-Symbolist" Hart Crane chose one such piece (a "mad speech" from Jonson's *The Alchemist*) as the epigraph to his long poem, "For the Marriage of Faustus and Helen":

> And so we may arrive by Talmud skill
> And profane Greek to raise the building up
> Of Helen's house against the Ismaelite,
> King of Thogarma, and his habergeons
> Brimstony, blue and fiery; and the force
> Of King Abaddon, and the beast of Cittim;
> Which Rabbi David Kimchi, Onkelos,
> And Aben Ezra do interpret Rome.

2. See Taupin, *l'Influence du symbolisme français sur la poésie américaine*, pp. 133-58, 275-78.

(1) *Name-allusions* ("le prince d'Aquitaine," "Lusignan"). Such uses of proper names, without gloss or elucidating context, imply that the person referred to is known to the reader. When this is not the case, the allusion produces Symbolism's feeling of withheld information. The best the reader can do is to extract whatever associations surround the name itself.

(2) *Apparent reference to an unknown story or symbolic value* ("la nuit du tombeau," "la fleur . . ."). Like name-allusions, such references imply unavailable knowledge through their specificity. They seem to allude to some particular occurrence or some figurative meaning of which the reader has no knowledge—hence the same feeling of mysteriousness.

(3) *Incompatible-union phrases* ("le soleil noir," "étoile morte"). These phrases are always based on an internal contradiction or incompatibility—the marriage of the concrete and the abstract, of the visual and the auditory, or simply a literal impossibility. Such a phrase is in a state of tension, and demands that equilibrium be restored by attributing to one or both of the words some iconographic meaning that will make them compatible. When none is available or when none seems preferable to others, the feeling of incomplete comprehension is again produced; the phrase cannot then work as a unit, but only as an evocative fragment.

Now, in Nerval's "El Desdichado" such frustrated allusions and implications of unknown lore occur in strings, which is another structural trait. The poem is a series of heterogeneous images and references, and the reader, guided by his notion of the speaker and the tone, moves from image to image, reacting to the evocative possibilities of each. While the string-of-allusions construction is quite common among Symbolist poems, it has its limitations. There must be a simplicity of subject and development if the poem is to be followed, yet this simplicity must not be so great as to make the poem tedious. Saint-Pol-Roux's "Liminaire," the opening poem in his collection *Les Reposoirs de la procession* (1893), illustrates one aspect of this problem:

Pèlerin magnifique en palmes de mémoire
(O tes pieds nus sur le blasphème des rouliers!)
Néglige les crachats épars dans le grimoire
Injuste des crapauds qui te sont des souliers.

Enlinceulant ta rose horloge d'existence,
Evoque ton fantôme à la table des fols
Et partage son aigle aux ailes de distance
Afin d'apprivoiser la foi des tournesols.

De là, miséricorde aux bons plis de chaumière
Avec un front de treille et la bouche trémière,
Adopte les vieux loups qui bèlent par les champs

Et régénère leur prunelle douloureuse
Au diamant qui rit dans la houille des temps
Comme l'agate en fleur d'une chatte amoureuse.
                                    (Message au poète adolescent.)

Roux's sonnet is an ideal starting-point, not only because it provides an excellent example of the Nervalian technique, but because, in so doing, it defines the limit of complexity in this technique as well. For the poem sits on the very outskirts of comprehension. When it is effective, when the reader can get a sense of some direction in the rhetoric, it is sublimely evocative. When direction is lost—as occurs at the end of the sonnet—it is nothing but a tangle of confused images, a poetic catalogue of flora and fauna gone wild.

The poem, according to Saint-Pol-Roux, is a "message au poète adolescent," and the young poet is not only the addressed party but the subject as well. He is exhorted, in successive sentences, to work toward fulfilling his destiny as a poet, and this exhortation is fivefold: *néglige, évoque, partage, adopte,* and *régénère.* This is the first and most basic bit of communication in the sonnet. Just as, in Nerval's

"El Desdichado," the succession of *Je suis* established a tone
of intense introspection, so here the succession of second-
person imperatives makes clear the speaker's intention (to
define the poet's path) and his tone (urging, encouraging).
This fact will order everything that follows.

What is the nature of the speaker's urging? The first quatrain is the clearest in import: the poet is at odds with his
immediate surroundings, and the speaker urges him to overlook the discomforts of this state. "At odds with" is repeated
twice in the same image. He is "barefoot on the blasphemy
of the truckers"; that is, his only shoes are the "sparse spittle
in the unjust scribblings of toads." [3] Meaning here arises
from nothing other than the disharmony of images. What the
"blasphème des rouliers" might be, or how the "crachats
épars dans le grimoire injuste des crapauds" can even be
imagined, is not relevant here. What is important is that they
come into contact with the bare feet of the poet—bare feet
meaning both "that which is vulnerable" and "that by which
one walks and goes forward." The young poet is urged to
overlook these obstacles as a barefoot walker overlooks peb-
bles and gravel in his path—a painful process, to be sure,
but one that is necessary to progression. And in the last
analysis, the obstructiveness of these obstacles does not seem
too much for the young poet. The reader's only glimpse of
him so far is as a "magnificent pilgrim" in a solemn, one-
man procession,[4] quite unmindful of everything around
him—the perfect embodiment of the speaker's command,
"Néglige."

Such is the paraphrasable content of the first quatrain.
What does its meaning arise from? The nouns and adjectives

3. My translation weakens this phrase because there is more lee-
way in *grimoire* and *crapauds* than in their translations, and because,
as in so much of Roux's work, images proceed here through sound
association (e.g. *crachats . . . crapaud*).

4. "En palmes de mémoire" not only suggests that memory, or
future ages, will bestow the accolades denied by the poet's own time,
but is reminiscent of *palmes académiques* and the associated solemn
processionals.

of this first sentence of the poem are arranged in a grammatical unit, and yet, on first reading, no unity of meaning is available. Since the sentence has the incomplete comprehension typical of unrecognized allusion, the reader is encouraged to seek an iconographic significance in some or all of the words, so that a unity of meaning may be retrieved. But if the sentence is literally impossible, it is also iconographically undirected. There is no lore surrounding *pieds nus, rouliers, crachats,* or *crapauds* that will restore to the sentence the kind of certainty to which we are accustomed in ordinary discourse. Thus the sentence fragments into a series of disjointed associations. In its most striking phrase, "les crachats épars dans le grimoire / Injuste des crapauds," an example of "incompatible union," the emergence of sense is as follows: *crachats* means "disgusting," "contempt," "crassness," "not particularly harmful," "on the ground," etc.; *épars* means "sparse," "not overwhelming"; *grimoire* means "not understood," "nonsensical"; *injuste* means "unfair"; and *crapauds* means "low," "despicable," "not particularly threatening" (furthermore, it is often applied as a contemptuous epithet to human beings). To reassemble these impressions into a unit of sense as well as one of grammar requires complete abandonment of the words of the text. Thus some of the associations of the last half of the quatrain might be ordered into: "Pay no attention to the crass contempt which will be at your feet; it will not be unmanageable, and it comes, after all, from the nonsensical and unfair ragings of low and despicable people." This is, of course, the folly of paraphrase, for such a version leaves out much of the "information" provided by the text's evocative references and removes that feeling of doubt, of vague shadowy communication, which is so important to the poem's effect. Roux's method, then, is one of fragmentation, just as is Nerval's in "El Desdichado," and as the poem continues, the difficulties mount.

The second quatrain still offers some meaningful content, although it is more obscure than the first. It is about the poet and time. Putting aside (literally "enshrouding," burying) his "pink clock of existence," the poet is urged to summon his own phantom [5] to "the table of madmen." [6] *Rose* here means "rosy," "comfortable," "pleasant" (cf. *voir la vie en rose*), and the notion introduced by *horloge* is that our normal existence carries with it a limited (comfortable) concept of time. The poet, however, is enjoined to meet his own immortal, timeless image face-to-face—to confront himself in eternity. [7] What takes place at this encounter (which is beyond the bounds of reason, "à la table des fols") has the semblance of some unknown ritual, the sharing of the phantom's "distance-winged eagle," in order to "tame [domesticate] the faith of the sunflowers." *Apprivoiser* means not only to tame, to bring into submission, but often to "establish a connection with," "to make one's own" as well. [8] As for the faith of the sunflowers (and here the reader is equipped with a bit of traditional lore), the meaning is a faith connected with cyclical time, with the perpetual rising and setting of the sun. Thus the putting aside of our normal, roseate time-clock in favor of a more abstract, far-seeing view of time (the sunflowers' faith) is the poet's task, and he accomplishes it through this strange ceremony with his own phantom. About the ceremony itself, little can be divined, but the proximity of *table, partage,* and *aigle* suggests an eerie meal, where the total fare is to be this indigestible, noble bird [9] with "wings of distance." Such rugged victuals

5. Alluding to the belief that every human being has, during his lifetime, his own phantom in the spiritual world with whom he is only united at the time of his earthly death.

6. For Roux's preference for the form *fol* (instead of *fou*), cf. his prose poem "Le Fol" in *Reposoirs de la procession,* vol. 1.

7. This necessity to free himself from his own time is the implication of *palmes de mémoire* in line 1.

8. "To tame," in the sense of "to gain mastery over," is *dompter* in French.

9. "Aigle" is another of the rare words in the text that have both a well-established iconographic significance and one that is relevant to the total image.

are, after all, in keeping with the rugged course enjoined by the speaker.

Saint-Pol-Roux's method in the second quatrain thus closely resembles the procedure in the first. Again, the reader is confronted, not with a unifiable chain of meanings, but with a series of fragmented impressions and associations. Meaning is framed in the strong tone established in the first quatrain and continued in the second, and emerges from sets of equivalences: just as *pieds nus* and *souliers* both establish the idea of "bare feet" (i.e. moving forward, possible pain, etc.) as central to the first stanza, so do *horloge* and *tournesol* point to a common, central idea in the second, that of time. And such reinforcements give a certain direction to the whole. It is chiefly through *horloge* and *tournesols* that the reader can perceive time to be the subject of the second quatrain, and it is through this perception that the associations hovering around *fantôme, aigle,* and *distance* can take shape.

Such is not the case with the rest of the poem. One might imagine that the evocation of the thatched hut (lines 9 and 10) is parallel to the speaker's previous urgings toward a rugged, individual life—an assumption supported by a familiarity with Roux's own biography.[10] If so, this theme seems to be continued in the following line, and in the final tercet there is a hinted parallelism in the series *prunelle-diamant-agate*—all hard, shiny, and small objects. But this is only conjecture. Lacking the unifying elements seen in the first two quatrains, the last six lines trail off into incomprehension. Indeed, not only is direction lacking in the images, but even the grammar (so important to establishing parallelisms and bridging associations) is ambiguous. It is not entirely clear whether the prepositions *aux* (line 9) and *au* (line 13) express an attributive or agentive relationship, or what *comme* (line 14) refers to. Given the already existing

10. In 1898 Roux himself settled down in a *chaumière* near Lanverzanel and stayed there for several years with his family (see Th. Briant, *Saint-Pol-Roux,* pp. 29-36).

disorder, these ambiguities cannot be productive. To be sure, the strong tone is still present (*adopte* and *régénère* give some definition), and the continuance of the themes of hardiness (lines 9–11) and condensation of time (lines 13 and 14) is suggested, but any real sense of direction is lacking. The reader senses the beginnings of some sort of meaning (largely because of the first two quatrains), but nothing emerges.

This, then, represents one limit in the technique of unrecognized references. In a poem constructed as a string of brilliant fragments, of one flashing association after the next, it is necessary that the direction-giving elements work throughout the poem, and that the poem's development remain rather simple. In "Liminaire" a well-defined subject (viz. "message au poète adolescent"), strong tone, clear grammatical relationships, parallelisms, and equivalencies in the imagery initially supply some direction to the evocative fragments. As they weaken and the complexity builds, the poem breaks down.

A poem of similar structure (but without Roux's problems) is Maeterlinck's "Oraison," from the collection *Serres chaudes:*

> Mon âme a peur comme une femme,
> Voyez ce que j'ai fait, Seigneur,
> De mes mains, les lys de mon âme,
> De mes yeux, les cieux de mon cœur!
>
> Ayez pitié de mes misères!
> J'ai perdu la palme et l'anneau:
> Ayez pitié de mes prières,
> Faibles fleurs dans un verre d'eau.
>
> Ayez pitié du mal des lèvres,
> Ayez pitié de mes regrets,
> Semez les lys le long des fièvres
> Et des roses sur les marais.
>
> Mon Dieu! d'anciens vols de colombes
> Jaunissent le ciel de mes yeux,

> Ayez pitié du lin des lombes
> Qui m'entoure de gestes bleus.[11]

One finds, in Maeterlinck's poem, the usual techniques of implying a significance unknown to the reader: phrases which appear to allude to some preestablished symbolic significance (e.g. "la palme et l'anneau") or the combination of words into an irreconcilable union (e.g. "gestes bleus," "le lys le long des fièvres"). To be sure, the poem is not as uniformly allusive as the Roux example, and there are many conventional-looking usages. Still, the poem is not lacking in mysteriousness.

What distinguishes this poem from "Liminaire," however, is the fact that its mysteriousness is far from overwhelming. The most important fact about the speaker is stated unequivocally in the first line: he is afraid in his soul, and the rest of the poem will be concerned with this spiritual anxiety. "Have pity," repeated five times in the text, establishes the tone just as unequivocally. Furthermore, the fact that this phrase is repeated indicates that the poem's strings of images will all be restatements of the same condition. However the images change, the theme, subject, and tone will remain constant.

Now, at the end of the poem there remain many things the reader does not know: what the speaker has lost (line 6),[12] what the doves or loincloth may symbolize, why the flower imagery is used, where the speaker's anxiety comes from, or even the general characteristics of this anxiety. Yet these uncertainties are hardly noticed. So strong is the tone, so simple the structure and the apparent subject, that the aura of mysteriousness and incomplete comprehension is not

11. Maeterlinck, *Poésies complètes*, pp. 123-24.
12. It must be noted, in fairness, that *palme* and *anneau* both have traditional iconographic significance, the former meaning "reward," "recognition of victory," and the latter "wedding." Yet there is no reinforcement of these meanings (contrast with the Housman example of "rose" and "laurel," above). The effective meaning of line 6 is: "I have lost something"; whether what has been lost is connected with success, victory, marriage, etc. can only be conjectured.

perceived as being particularly oppressive, which accounts for the poem's limitations as well as its virtues. To the extent that the reader is made to feel—rightly or wrongly—that he has grasped the essential, the poem's evocative phrases are purely gratuitous. If there is nothing compelling about the poem's incomprehension, then its strangeness is somehow irrelevant.

Whether this is true of Maeterlinck's "Oraison" out of context is another question. In context—that is, in *Serres chaudes,* where it appears alongside half a dozen poems on the same subject and of similar simplicity—the poem's mysteries lose some of their power. If a clear subject and tone, restatement through parallelisms, unambiguous grammar, and so forth are necessary to give the poem direction (as was seen in "Liminaire"), they may not be so self-sufficient as to eliminate the necessity of seeking some meaning in the allusive usages.

Between these two poles lie some of the best poems of Symbolism. The following, for example, is from Rimbaud's "Alchimie du Verbe" (*Une Saison en Enfer*):

> Le loup criait sous les feuilles
> En crachant les belles plumes
> De son repas de volailles:
> Comme lui je me consume.
>
> Les salades, les fruits
> N'attendent que la cueillette;
> Mais l'arraignée de la haie
> Ne mange que des violettes.
>
> Que je dorme! Que je bouille
> Aux autels de Solomon.
> Le bouillon court sur la rouille,
> Et se mêle au Cédron.[13]

13. Rimbaud, *Œuvres complètes*, p. 232.

The poem's restatable content is small. Its first "ordering statement" occurs in the fourth line: like this wolf, spitting up the feathers from his meal, the speaker is "wasting away." *Je me consume* is almost a pun. For although *se consumer,* when used in regard to people, is rarely taken literally, it almost takes on this literal meaning, given all the other eating and consuming going on in the poem. But the way the speaker "consumes himself" is the way the wolf does, and in either case the poem is talking about a state of mind; it is represented in the wolf's action. What, then, is the significance of this act, this spitting out of the *belles plumes?*

The following stanza presents another version of the same action and thus the beginnings of an answer. "Salads, fruits" (the words are intentionally drab and devoid of color) "wait only to be picked." Instead, what is consumed are the violets, this stanza's parallel to "belles plumes." In neither image is the reader tempted to accept the description at face value. That is, he does not attribute the speaker's discontent to these two happenings alone, but sees them as symptoms, somehow representative or referential. Yet what they represent cannot be stated. Clearly, one meaning that emerges from *violettes* and *belles plumes* is "delicate, colorful, beautiful," and there is the temptation to interpret the two images as representing the destruction of beautiful things. But the poem does not permit oversimplification. Those associations may be undeniably present in the speaker's discontent, but so is the notion of wastefulness. The wolf cannot eat the beautiful feathers; he spits them out and howls. Similarly, the spider wastes potential salads and fruits in favor of what, at least to the reader, appears to be a much less tempting meal. There is something wrong about this, something out of order. And connected with it is the idea of self-destruction. In his "repas de volailles" the wolf is feeding on his own kind, another animal—there is a sense of self-destruction even in that—so that the natural world *se consume* (literally) the way the speaker does (figuratively).

Rimbaud's treatment of transition here is of prime importance in understanding the poem's mysteriousness. The transitional words "Comme lui" (line 4) and "Mais" (line 7) trigger the reader's sense of incomprehension. They imply a relationship that is not immediately apparent, and it is precisely this implication that brings the reader to look for some special significance in the images surrounding these transition points. In other words, the unrecognized relationships carried in "comme" and "mais" make the wolf, the feathers, the spider, and the violets into "apparent references to an unknown story or symbolic value." From these fragments and the vaguely perceived parallelisms derive the notions of beauty destroyed and wasted, of things consuming themselves.

All these associations, contained in the two images, move the speaker to the exclamations of the third stanza, "Que je dorme! Que je bouille!" The two exclamations are grammatical parallels and suggest a common meaning, the desire for death. "Autels de Salomon" is not an invented phrase (it occurs in the Bible, Chronicles II), but its function in the poem is, of course, nonreferential. It is a name-allusion. "Altars" means, in effect, "ceremony," "death," "sacrifice," and so on, while Solomon means "wisdom," "the Bible," and related associations. Occurring where it does in the poem, this connection of the speaker with a ritual, biblical death is seen as a resolution of the speaker's anxiety. He separates himself from the first two stanzas rhetorically (with the abrupt interjection), spatially (with the evocation first of Solomon, then of the biblical river Cedron), and temporally. And having removed himself, he is reduced to a bubbling froth that drips down the "rust" (decay, waste) into the eternal stream. What moves him to desire this ritual merging lies among the evocative fragments of the first two stanzas: in the destruction of beautiful things, in life destroying life, in wasteful inappropriateness.

Single Image

Beyond the poems of "string-of-allusions" construction there is another important group of Symbolist poems—a group which logically (but not historically) grows out of the first. It contains poems that are made, not of strings of allusions, but of a single allusive phrase or image, stated and restated as the poem moves on, commented on, reacted to, defined in different contexts. This single, central enigma is thus analytically no different from those already considered, and the same demands of tone, subject matter, and restatement are in force—perhaps more so than before, since the poem cannot rely on parallelisms and equivalencies between images, but must rest its entire fate on one image elaborated and discussed in different contexts. The best way to grasp the structure of such a poem is to look at specific examples. The following is by the Russian Symbolist, Zinaida Gippius:—

Возня

Остов разложившейся собаки
Ходит вкруг летящего ядра.
Долго ли тереть мне эти знаки?
Кончится ли подлая игра?

Все противно в них: соединенье,
И согласный, соразмерный ход,
И собаки тлеющей крученье,
И ядра бессмысленный полет.

Если б мог собачий труп остаться,
Ярко пламенным столбом сгореть!
Если б одному ядру умчаться
Одному свободно умереть!

Но в мирах надзвездных нет событий,
Все летит, летит безвольный ком
И крепки вневременные нити:
Песий труп вертится за ядром.

Hubbub

Now the skeleton of the rotted dog
Runs around the cannon's flying ball.
How long must I bear such auguries?
Will the cheap play never end at all?

Everything about them gives offense
As the pair moves, unified in rite:
Dog that circles . . . circles as he rots,
Ball without a meaning to its flight.

If the dog's dead body could stand still
And burn up in flames—pillared, bright, high!
If the ball could fly away somewhere
By itself and being free just die!

In the upper star-world—no events,
And the will-less mass flies, flies withal. . .
And the timeless threads cannot be torn.
So the dog's cadaver hounds the ball.[14]

The central image of the poem, the dog's carcass that circles
the ball, is an impossibility, an internal contradiction. And
taken as such, it is unknowable, totally foreign to the reader's
linguistic experience. As a consequence, it cannot exist as a
unit. Because the dog cannot *be* with the flying ball, the
phrase falls apart. The reader's attention moves from the
image itself to connotations and associations belonging to the
individual component words. Around *tlejuščij* (rotting),*trup*
(corpse), etc., group the ideas of death, repugnance, and
decay; to this is added contempt connected with *sobaka*
(dog) and, especially, *pës* (cur). The act of circling around
the ball (a cannonball, presumably) is reminiscent of the
earth's rotation around the sun, eternal and unstoppable,
and these associations cling to the image as well.

Now the poem's tone is outlined in some detail. It is not,
as one might expect, shock or incomprehension. The speaker

14. Translated in Vl. Markov and M. Sparks, *Modern Russian
Poetry*, p. 78.

makes it quite clear that the image has meaning (*znaki,* "signs," line 3) and reacts to it first with annoyance (stanza 1), disgust (stanza 2), yearning for its cessation (stanza 3), and resignation to its eternal continuance (stanza 4). It is the strength of this reaction that keeps the poem's mysteriousness from becoming mystification. That is, the reader cannot resign himself with the thought, "This is an uncomprehensible happening," since clearly the speaker sees some significance in it which enables him to react so violently against it. But what in the image produces this reaction?

That which is *protivno,* "offensive" (and the root of the word "against" is to be emphasized), is the harmonious combination of ball and corpse—and in Russian the statement almost sounds like an oxymoron, nearly: "What's so contrary is their agreement." It is this "harmonious, well-balanced" flight that the speaker finds so repulsive. Now, although initially the image seems anything but harmonious, the poem's insistence on this quality, on the unchanging nature of the apparition, is finally convincing. This new association—harmonious—takes its place next to the qualities of inevitability and eternity already felt in the image.

The same smooth, fruitless eternity is echoed in another part of Gippius's picture. The dog is, after all, dead, yet he is somehow required to continue this cheap game, the endless circling. His existence should be over, yet he still goes on, decomposing but circling all the same. For in the poem the sentence of death that hangs over all things has been suspended. It is as if all takes place in interstellar space— no gravity, no air, no "events," only eternal, senseless motion. The ball flies endlessly toward no target, the dog circles endlessly around the ball. And so the speaker's reaction becomes clearer, and with it, the import of the image. It is this utterly foreign perfection, this wholly inhuman harmony that arouses such contempt in the speaker. In such a world death is an expression, not of submission to natural law, but of individual (N.B. *odnomu . . . odnomu*) freedom; and death is, of course, inconceivable.

By the end of the poem the reader is able to feel something of the speaker's violent reaction and to experience the image's repugnance himself, and yet the mysteriousness remains. In the concluding stanza the reader still does not know where the image comes from, what it means, or what it may refer to; he only knows how to react to it or, more precisely, which of the associations it evokes are relevant to its still-veiled significance. What the dog is or was, what meaning is to be given to *jadro* (ball)—these are questions he still cannot answer.

The central image of "Hubbub" is structurally of the same order as the type *soleil noir:* an internal contradiction, a defiance of logic and nature. Obviously, many poems built around a single phrase or image might use this particular technique of strangeness, such as Wallace Stevens's "The Emperor of Ice-Cream," which has as its main phrase another irreconcilable union ("emperor of ice-cream"). Yeats's "The Collar-bone of a Hare" is built around an implied but unknown symbolic value (viz. the title)—the same technique as was seen in Nerval's phrase "La fleur qui plaisait tant" or Maeterlinck's "la palme et l'anneau." Poems written around a central image use any such allusive forms, each of which, as has been seen, is capable of producing the uncertainty and strangeness sought by the Symbolists.

Grammatical Chaos

In the poems already examined, it has been seen that a clear notion of the grammatical relationship between consecutive phrases and clauses is important in establishing equivalencies between images. Often the prepositions and conjunctions which establish these relationships are important in indicating shifts in tone as well. In a particularly dense poem, such as Roux's "Liminaire," the reader's failure to grasp grammatical and syntactical relationships can contribute to the poem's loss of direction. In many Symbolist poems, then, the clarity of grammatical and syntactic parallels may be seen to prevent the obscurity of unrecognized names, internally contradictory phrases, and the like from becoming a total obscurity.

There exist, however, a number of Symbolist poems (most of them written by Mallarmé), in which grammar and syntax become intentionally obscure—poems in which, in addition to the techniques of strangeness already analyzed, there are the further difficulties of confusing word order, ambiguous relationships between clauses, separation of noun and adjective, noun and verb, and so forth. In such cases something has to give. Often it is the complexity of the subject (many of Mallarmé's poems are immensely complicated statements of rather simple ideas, or merely descriptions of an object, a landscape, etc.). Otherwise, it is the density of allusive phrases that must be sacrificed. And, occasionally, it is the reader.

Mallarmé's "Soupir," first published in the 1866 volume of *Le Parnasse Contemporain,* is an excellent example of Mallarmé's chaotic word-order working within the frame of a wholly schematic, simple subject.

> Mon âme vers ton front où rêve, ô calme sœur,
> Un automne jonché de tachcs de rousseur,
> Et vers le ciel errant de ton œil angélique
> Monte, comme dans un jardin mélancolique,
> Fidèle, un blanc jet d'eau soupire vers l'Azur!
> —Vers l'Azur attendri d'octobre pâle et pur
> Qui mire aux grands bassins sa langueur infinie
> Et laisse, sur l'eau morte où la fauve agonie
> Des feuilles crre au vent et creuse un froid sillon,
> Se traîner le soleil jaune d'un long rayon.[15]

The subject is a gesture, an upward motion going from the speaker to the "you" of the poem. It is paralleled in the motion of a fountain "sighing" toward the sky on an autumn day. But to say that the action is paralleled is to do the poem

15. S. Mallarmé, *Poésies* (Paris, 1945) p. 41.

an injustice, for the speaker is completely identified with the
fountain and the "you" with the sky. Epithets applied to the
fountain belong to the speaker, verbs belonging to the sky
describe an action of the "you," and so forth. The result of
this grand exercise in hypallage are expressions that, at first
glance, look like the internal contradictions and incompatible unions already discussed: *un automne rêve* (*dans*) *ton
front, le ciel errant de ton œil, la fauve agonie des feuilles.*
They do not, however, possess the compelling elusiveness
seen in previous poems; and once the critical insight of ad-
jectival and verbal transposition is gained, their obscurity
disappears. In the end, then, the poem is not unresolvable.
It is possible to rearrange the components, change the word
order, and produce a coherent, synthetic statement of the
speaker, the spoken-to, and the landscape.

To do so, however, is to work against the poem. What is
elusive and mysterious about it (although not permanently
so) is the fusion created by the cross-distribution of epithets,
and this fusion is maintained by the difficulty in "breaking
the poem down"—that is, by its difficult word-order. The
fusion is such that the poem is a complete act of polariza-
tion: on the one hand, the mounting, sighing "moi" (or his
alter-ego, the fountain), and on the other, the responsive
"toi" (or the sky). Every quality or action in the poem can
be ascribed to one of these two poles.

But even this view of the poem—which subsumes everything in it under one of two categories—does not show fully
the union created. For the gesture of the poem itself is that
of fusion between these two poles, *moi* and *toi*. They reach
out and correspond to each other, and this is represented in
the poet's giving parallel bits of information about each of
them. We know:

(1) Persons involved:	*moi*	*toi, ô calme sœur*
(2) More specifically:	*mon âme*	*ton front, ton œil*
(3) The purity associated with them:	*blanc jet d'eau*	*l'Azur, angélique*
(4) And the immensity:	*grands bassins*	*ciel errant*

(5) Their autumn mood:	*eau morte, fauve*	*automne jonché,*
	agonie des feuilles	*octobre pâle et pur*
(6) And its langor:	*jardin mélanco-*	*langueur infinie*
	lique	
(7) Their attitude toward each other:	*fidèle*	*attendri*
(8) And the gesture which expresses it:	*monte, soupire*	*mire, laisse se traîner*

So, in the end, the grammatical chaos justifies itself. If the obscure word-order helps to make of the poem one blurred set of impressions in which it is not wholly clear which epithet applies to what, it is performing the act of fusion which is the poem's subject and theme. In this dimly perceived scene a reader can sense the same unity that becomes apparent in a systematic breakdown of the poem. Furthermore, he has a very real sense of the poem's strangeness, which comes from not quite understanding what is being done by whom. Moreover, the climactic word-order at the end of the poem (two lines separate "laisse" from its complementary infinitive and predicate) gives great emotional force to the last line, and yet this force only raises answerable questions: What is its significance? Who is the speaker? To whom or what is he speaking?

To a certain extent Mallarmé's poem is mysterious in the same way as Nerval's or Rimbaud's. Some of its enigmatic quality arises from the "incompatible-union" phrases already seen. Furthermore, like these other poems, "Soupir" becomes meaningful only through fragmentation: the reader must "destroy" the poem in order to grasp significant parallels. But the unity of "Soupir" also recalls Gippius's "Hubbub." The single action of the poem, a soul climbing up toward the brow of this "calme sœur," unites on the same plane that which is physical with that which is not. As with Gippius, it is the apparent disharmony of the central image that calls into question the poem itself and implies that our knowledge of the action or actors is somehow insufficient.

Motive

There exists a type of Symbolist poem which presents no initial incoherence—one which has neither strings of unrecognized or impossible images, nor a single allusive image, nor (as seen in Mallarmé) apparent internal contradictions in a grammatically unclear framework. On the contrary, this kind of Symbolist poem presents a wholly coherent utterance, without any of the lexical or grammatical friction observed thus far. But when such poems are successful, they produce the same feeling of withheld information and incomprehension as other Symbolist poems. It arises, not from incoherence, but from an inability to understand *motive*. An action or series of actions is fully grasped in its description (everything described is literally possible, imaginable, and totally comprehensible), but the reader still cannot know what is going on because he does not know why it is going on. A phrase which can serve as a suitable model for this type of poem is Eliot's "Midnight shakes the memory / As a madman shakes a dead geranium" (from "Rhapsody on a Windy Night"), where the comparison gains its strength not only from the violence of the image but from its incomprehensibility as well. The madman's act is at once possible and inscrutable.

A number of things may be asserted about such inscrutable-motive poems. First, they are, among the types discussed, the least "uniquely Symbolist"; that is, one may find examples of such poems in pre-Symbolist writings.[16] They are, moreover, a clear departure from the frustrated-allusion technique (even though such usages do occasionally appear in such poems). The only *lore* that is alluded to is the reader's understanding of human behavior, and it is questioned, cast aside, or contradicted in the action of the poem. "Motive

16. Particularly among some of the English poets of the Romantic period—Blake, Coleridge, and Browning. (The latter's "Childe Rowland to the Dark Tower Came" is an extended example of this sort of poem.)

poems" are rather severely limited in subject matter (since strangeness issues not only from method of presentation but from the subject as well), and often have the trappings of the gothic novel: eerie landscape, preoccupation with death, anticipation, and so on.[17] Furthermore, such poems are most often epigrammatic in structure, with the last line either stating or summarizing the inscrutable act—this is almost always necessary in order to make the mysteriousness the most compelling and important aspect of the poem.

The following poem by Fëdor Sologub is a good example of this particular subgenre:

> Порой повеет запах странный, —
> Его причины не понять, —
> Давно померкший, день туманный
> Переживается опять.
>
> Как встарь, опять печально всходишь
> На обветшалое крильцо,
> Засов скрипучий вновь отводишь,
> Вращая ржавое кольцо, —
>
> И видишь тесные покои,
> Где половицы чуть скрипят,
> Где отсырелые обои
> В углах тихонько шелестят,
>
> Где скучный маятник маячит,
> Внимая скучным, злым речам,
> Где кто-то молится да плачет
> Так долго плачет по ночам.[18]

17. The Russian Symbolists, particularly Belyj, excelled in this mode. E.g. "Predčuvstvie" [Foreboding], "Na skate" [On the Slope], "S vysoty" [From the heights], and "Xuliganskaja Pesen'ka" [A Hooligan's Jingle]—all in A. Belyj, *Stixotvorenija i Po'emy*.

18. At times a strange smell comes wafting—impossible to know its cause; faded long ago, the misty day lives again. As of old, again you sadly walk up the decrepit steps and pull back the squeaky bolt, turning the rusted ring,—And you see the narrow rooms, where the floorboards squeak, where damp wallpaper rustles quietly in the corners—Where the tedious pendulum swings, harkening to tedious,

The scene floats in on this *zapax strannyj,* and it is perhaps an actual "strange scent" that brings the speaker into contact with his past. (The "you" in the poem is, in both Russian and English, merely second-person in form; the speaker is talking about himself.) In any case, it is clear that what is happening in the poem is the reliving of some distant day (line 4). The description of this day, however eerie or spooky it may be, is not incoherent. Indeed, the things described have a familiar ring for those schooled in ghost stories and the like: the creaking latch, the squeaky floorboards, the rust, the must, the sound of pendulum—these are almost clichés. While the poem may produce Symbolism's typical sense of withheld information, this feeling does not arise from an inability to deal with the language of the poem. Rather, the mystery arises from the action described in the last two lines. The sounds are not necessarily part of the "ghost-story" cliché, but only praying and crying—sounds very much of this world and made by a real person. Whoever that person is—the speaker as a boy, or someone from his family—the repeated action, the nightly crying, is what ultimately cannot be explained. By its position in the poem and by the repetition of *plačet* (crying) it is clearly not only the most important part of the scene but the real raison d'être of the entire description; and yet the reader knows nothing of what provokes it. As in other Symbolist poems, it can be reacted to but not quite understood.

It is not unusual that poems of this type employ some of the other techniques of strangeness already seen, albeit in a less compelling and dense fashion. The following, by Maurice Maeterlinck (quite typical of his later style), shows such a mixture of devices:

> Les sept filles d'Orlamonde,
> Quand la fée fut morte,
> Les sept filles d'Orlamonde,
> Cherchèrent les portes.

---

evil talk, where someone is praying and crying, crying so long at night.—F. Sologub, *Sobrannie Sočinenia,* 1 : 60.

Ont allumé leurs sept lampes,
Ont ouvert les tours,
Ont ouvert quatre cent salles,
Sans trouver le jour. . .

Arrivent aux grottes sonores,
Descendent alors;
Et sur une porte close,
Trouvent une clef d'or.

Voient l'océan par les fentes,
Ont peur de mourir,
Et frappent à la porte close,
Sans oser l'ouvrir. . .[19]

As was seen in Chapter 1, most of Maeterlinck's poetry after *Serres chaudes* has the resonance of folk myth, and it is not unusual to find in his later works unrecognized names (Orlamonde), an abundance of numbers, and rather traditional symbols (the lamps, the golden key) whose iconographical significance is neither supported nor refuted by the context. What is most compelling in the scene, however, is not the unrecognized names or the implied symbolic values but the final action taken by the seven girls. What they see through the cracks in the door is the sea, which is immediately linked with the fear of death. Yet they are standing on the inside looking out, and if they see the sea through the cracks, they have come to the end of their search for daylight, *le jour*. Their hesitation arises from fear and a contrary impulse to fling open the door and meet the daylight they have been looking for. What results is this wholly senseless act: they knock on the door from the inside, as if entreating someone or something to open it, while the key that can unlock it

19. Maeterlinck, *Poésies complètes*, pp. 191-92. Maeterlinck adapted this song for use in his play *Ariane et Barbe-bleue*, and in this context the keys, the locked doors, etc., must be considered in conjunction with those of the play itself. However, it is clear that the song was written well before the play, and without any particular context other than the poems of "Quinze Chansons" which surround it. See J. Hanse's introduction to *Poésies complètes*, pp. 60-61.

remains in their possession, unused. The mixture of anxiety and anticipation on reaching the end of a search is not unfamiliar to most people, but it is nonetheless an inscrutable ambivalence—an ambivalence that finds its ideal expression in the last, totally useless act of the poem.

In this examination of motive-centered poems I have considered those in which the central action is set forth within a narrative framework. There are others, however, in which the poem itself is the act under consideration and the speaker of the poem is the whole source of its mysteriousness. Here, tone and persona are again crucial—not as redeemers of the poem's direction, but as the source of its strangeness. Consider, for example, Valerij Brjusov's celebrated "The Coming Huns":

ГРЯДУЩИЕ ГУННЫ

> Толчи их рай, Атилла!
> — Вяч. Иванов

Где вы, грядущие гунны,
Что тучей нависли над миром!
Я слышу ваш топот чугунный
По еще не открытым Памирам.

На нас ордой опьянелой
Рухните с темных становий —
Одивить одряхлевшее тело
Волной пылающей крови.

Поставте, невольники воли,
Шалаши у дворцов, как бывало,
Всколосите веселое поле
На месте тронного зала.

Сложите книги кострами,
Пляшите в их радостном свете,
Творите мерзость во храме, —
Вы во всем неповинны, как дети!

А мы, мудрецы и поеты,
Хранители тайны и веры,
Унесем зажженные свети
В катакомбы, в пустыни, в пещеры.

И что, под бурей летучей,
Под этой грозой разрушений,
Сохранит играющий Случай
Из наших заветных творений?

Бесследно все сгибнет, быть может,
Что ведомо было одним нам,
Но вас, кто меня уничтожит,
Встречаю приветственным гимном.

The Coming Huns

Tread on their Eden, Atilla!
V. Ivanov

Where are you Huns who are coming,
Who cloud the wide world with your spears?
I hear your pig iron tramping
On the still-undiscovered Pamirs.

Like a drunken horde from dark field-camps
Fall on us in a clamoring flood. . .
To revive our too-soon-grown-old bodies
With a fresh surge of burning blood.

Come on, you captives of freedom,
Pitch your tents by the palace wall.
As of old, make a gay field of ripe grain
On the site of the King's throne hall.

Burn all the books in bonfires,
Dance in their lighthearted light.
Be evil and base in the temples.
You are innocent in all you ignite.

And we, thinkers and poets and keepers
Of mysteries and faiths we would save,
Will carry away burning torches
To catacombs, to the desert and cave.

And what of our dear creations
In the winged storm's ferment,
In this thunderstorm of destruction,
Will be spared by amused Accident?

Perhaps all that is our own will perish
And leave no trace that men's eyes can see
Still I welcome with a hymn of greeting
All of you who will destroy me.[20]

The incomprehensible action of Brjusov's poem is the utter-
ing of the poem itself. It is essentially a single, simple statement, the speaker's call for the cataclysmic destruction of
himself, his country, and his culture. One critic has called
the poem a statement in which Brjusov "proclaims the thrill
of destruction as an end in itself," and there is some truth
in this.[21] Destruction is a thrilling thing in the poem, and
the reader cannot help but feel some of that thrill. Yet the
overwhelming fact of the poem is not destruction but self-
destruction, and this is its central mystery, recapitulated in
the last stanza. It is perhaps because the urge to self-
destruction is present in many people that the poem can be
such a compelling utterance. It should be noted at the outset,
however, that if the sentiment is familiar to the reader, it is
still inexplicable: it can be recognized but not understood.

The poem offers some arguments for self-destruction. The
speaker associates his own annihilation and that of his country with rebirth and revival (*oživit'*, stanza 2). His destroy-

20. Translation by Markov and Sparks, *Modern Russian Poetry*,
pp. 47-49.
21. C. M. Bowra, in his introduction to Vj. Ivanov, *Svet večernyj*,
p. 21. Bowra sees the poem as a corruption of the theme of artistic
freedom, the freedom to destroy, proclaimed in Ivanov's own *"Kočev-
niki Krasoty,"* from which Brjusov's epigraph is taken.

ers, like children, cannot be guilty of what they do (stanza 4), and their "youth" is in sharp contrast to the *mudricy i po'ety* (sages and poets) of the following line. The return is not only to innocence but to the past as well (*kak byvalo,* stanza 3), a restoration. Yet these are only arguments. What is the crime of age, in a society or a human being, and what is the speaker's guilt in being a seer or poet? There is nothing negative in his treatment of what is to be destroyed —*merzost'* ("atrocities"), the most unequivocal negative of the poem, applies to the Huns—and yet the speaker is constant in his urging of annihilation.

The mystery of the poem, then, ultimately returns to the character of the speaker. Who is he? The notion that he is a historical personage, a representative of the civilization overrun by the Huns in the fifth century, must be discarded. It is contradicted by his opening question, "Where are you?" He knows of the invasion and yet it has not taken place; he knows of the Pamirs and yet they have not been discovered. No, he is a speaker of today who either relives the invasion vicariously or (more likely) invites a new one of unknown, allegorical Huns. And so the poem returns to the initial question, his invitation to destruction, which cannot be answered. Even in an age that knows all about masochism, the reader's sense of withheld information is quite real, for the speaker's internal contradiction can only be named, never resolved. The whole focus of the poem is on the Huns, and yet its mysteriousness—indeed, its real subject—lies not in them but in the singer of this hymn of greeting.

A large number of Symbolist poems are structurally similar to Brjusov's "The Coming Huns"—for example, many of those in Blok's early "Fair Lady" cycle. The following is his celebrated "Presentiment of You":

> И тяжкий сон житейского сознанья
> Ты отряхнешь, тоскуя и любя.
> — Вл. Соловев

Предчувствую Тебя. Года проходят мимо —
Все в облике одном предчувствую Тебя.

Весь горизонт в огне — и ясен нестерпимо,
И молча жду, — тоскуя и любя.

Весь горизонт в огне, и близко появленье,
Но страшно мне: изменишь облик Ты,

И дерзкое возбудишь подозренье,
Сменив в конце привычные черты.

О как паду — и горестно, и низко,
Не одолев смертельные мечты!

Как ясен горизонт! И лучезарность близко.
Но страшно мне: изменишь облик Ты.[22]

The epigraph usually printed with the poem is from Vladimir
Solovëv: "You shall shake off the heavy sleep of everyday
consciousness, in anguish and in love," and this last phrase,
repeated in the second stanza of the text, is at the heart of
the speaker's mood. *Toska,* or in this case the verbal *toskuja,*
is not really anguish or anxiety, but a general state of in-
completeness, of being unfulfilled. The speaker is filled with
anticipation—a lover's anticipation—yet his attitude is
strangely self-subjugating, almost feminine. This is all that
is given. A knowledge of Solovëv's cult of Sophia, Divine

22.
   I sense Your coming. The years pass by—still
   of the same countenance I sense Your coming.

   The whole horizon is aflame, and unbearably clear,
   in silence I wait—in anguish and in love.

   The whole horizon is aflame, and close the apparition,
   But I am afraid: Your countenance may change,

   And, having changed Your familiar features after all,
   You will arouse impudent suspicions.

   Oh how I'll fall—sadly and low,
   Having failed to overcome my mortal dreams!

   How bright the horizon! And close the radiance.
   But I am afraid: Your countenance may change.

   —A. A. Blok, *Polnoe Sobrannie Stixotvorenij*
   (Moscow, 1952), 1 : 54.

Wisdom, and familiarity with other poems in the cycle will provide more background insight into the poem's origin, but the mystery of the speaker's state of mind remains. What is the basis for his fears (that she will "change her familiar features"), and what is the higher reality the speaker alludes to by implication in the epigraph and in the tenth line? These cannot be known, for, as in the Brjusov poem, the central mystery of the poem, the speaker, is only treated indirectly.

There is already, in Blok's poem, a certain indissolubility of the speaker and the subject: what the reader does not know about the speaker derives from what he does not know about the Lady. The speaker brings himself into question by asking questions about the Lady. Thus, in spite of all that it says, the poem leaves everything unsaid: not only is the speaker's state of mind unexplainable, but so is that which initially brings it about.

Precisely the same structure appears in a very beautiful poem by Wallace Stevens, "Some Friends from Pascagoula":

> Tell me more of the eagle, Cotton,
> And you, Black Sly,
> Tell me how he descended
> Out of the morning sky.
>
> Describe with deepened voice
> And noble imagery
> His slowly-falling round,
> Down to the fishy sea.
>
> Here was a sovereign sight
> Fit for a kinky clan.
> Tell me again of the point
> At which the flight began,
>
> Say how his heavy wings,
> Spread on the sun-bronzed air,
> Turned tip and tip away,
> Down to the sand, the glare

Of the pine trees edging the sand,
Dropping in sovereign rings
Out of his fiery lair.
Speak of the dazzling wings.[23]

The unrecognized name-allusions (Cotton, Black Sly—the
friends from Pascagoula, one might suppose) should not be
an obstacle to the reader. They occur, as has been seen in
other Symbolist poems, to establish an initial sense of partial
incomprehension and mystery. But the real drama is again
the speaker. For him the simplest thing in the world, the
flight of an eagle and its descent to earth, is filled with overwhelming significance. It is all he talks about, and even after
five stanzas everything remains unsaid. While the series of
imperatives—"Tell me," "Describe," "Tell me again,"
"Say," "Speak"—makes the poem's tone almost painfully compelling, it is impossible to know what there is in the bird's
flight, or in Cotton and Sly's retelling of it, that can arouse
this urgency. To be sure, there are suggestions: sovereignty,
nobility, brilliance; yet these are all undercut by the last
line. If that were all, then it has been already said by the
speaker and there would be no need for its retelling. On the
contrary, there is something in the speaker's mind (concern-
ing the flight itself or the retelling of the flight) that is not
being said, perhaps because it cannot be said. The poem is
in a state of continuous tension, the tension of having to
know and being unable to know.

Strangeness and Newness

Having to know and being unable to know characterizes
all the various Symbolist poems discussed in this chapter;
it is a statement of their essential method. Now, poets and
critics have been shouting up "strangeness" for a long time.
Perhaps the most persistent shouters of late have been the
Russian Formalist critics, who proclaimed *ostranenie*
("strangifying") as the cornerstone of all imaginative litera-

23. Wallace Stevens, *Poems*, pp. 68-69.

ture.[24] But for these critics, as for others, strangeness is nearly synonymous with newness, and, as has been pointed out, there is nothing novel about that kind of strangeness in poetry.[25]

The quality seen in the poems of Roux or Rimbaud, Gippius or Sologub, is of another order. For as we have seen, the strangeness of Symbolist poetry is identified with mysteriousness—in other words, not only that which had been previously unknown, but that which is unable to be fully understood, that which perpetually lies just beyond our grasp. The difference is great. Where a poetry of newness says, "You did not see before," a poetry of strangeness asserts, "You do not see." Whatever its preferred subjects, themes, or artistic creeds, a poetry of this kind always has the same refrain: that the most basic structure people hold in common, language, is not held in common at all. To the extent that such a poetry can have meaning, to the extent that we can participate in its unfolding, it is a triumph of our ability to sense emotion in tone or to grasp fundamental similarities and parallels. It is, for all that, a triumph in the midst of incomprehension—a victory in a world where, as readers, our own uncertainty and separateness is being established in the same breath.

24. See Viktor Šklovskij's article "Iskusstvo kak priëm" [Art as Device], in *Po'etika: sborniki po teorii po'etičeskovo jazyka,* pp. 112 and ff.

25. Victor Erlich, *Russian Formalism,* p. 179, makes this observation specifically in regard to the Formalists' *ostranenie,* citing the previous praise of strangeness in poetry by Aristotle, Coleridge, Wordsworth, and, more recently, the Surrealists.

5. Symbolism "Wanes"

A literary school begins. Young poets group around an older, acknowledged leader; they establish, or take over, a literary review of their own; and the movement gains momentum. Then, almost imperceptibly, it begins to falter. The press, having ceased its ridicule, launches into "historical" analyses of the school's rise to power; it is analyzed from within and without, reexamined, "rejuvenated," and slowly it begins to fade. The fading can result from the rise of a new school with new doctrines or simply from a loss of interest among younger poets.

Before discussing the "waning" of Symbolism, one must define the term. Waning is to be equated, not with total disappearance, but with loss of vitality. As was stated earlier in this study, the various Symbolist "schools" are particularly difficult to delimit: one might easily extend the French school, via Valéry and Claudel, into the 1930s, and the Anglo-American "school" still further. It is nonetheless possible, independent of this fact, to think of the moment of waning in the Symbolist schools as that moment when the values of the Symbolists—in their slogans and their poetry— began to lose their force as a rallying point for young poets. Michaud speaks of Symbolism, in its heyday, as the functional *âme collective* of young poets throughout France and other European countries.[1] The moment it ceased to have this effect, when the word *Symbolism* lost its magic, was the moment its decline began.

In France this probably occurred somewhere between 1894 and 1898, the latter marking the date of Mallarmé's death. Décaudin supports this thesis and seems himself to point to the year 1895.[2] Among the new directions characterizing French poetry at the time were movements to

---

1. G. Michaud, *Message poétique du symbolisme,* 3 : 471. Michaud is, I think, mistaken in extending this *âme collective* function all the way into the late 1890s.

2. Décaudin, *Crise des valeurs symbolistes,* pp. 27, 94-95.

"Naturism," nihilism, and a poetry of whimsy, as well as a new interest in social engagement—the latter spurred by the Dreyfus affair and Zola's *J'accuse,* published on January 13, 1898. In any case, five years later the decline of Symbolism had become an open topic. Cornell cites an article by Léon Vannoz published in 1903 which stated categorically that Symbolism, at least as a school, had ceased to exist. In addition, quoting from a literary poll taken in 1901, he shows the place young poets of the day, even then, accorded to the Symbolists. In answer to the question "Quel est votre poète?" the 120 responding poets selected, in descending order, Victor Hugo, Alfred de Vigny, Verlaine, Baudelaire, Larmartine, Musset, Leconte de Lisle, and Mallarmé.[3] The fact that Mallarmé, the acknowledged *chef d'ecole* of the Symbolists, comes so low on the list is something of an indictment of the entire school—and one that certainly would not have been made ten years earlier.[4]

There were, to be sure, people who claimed the contrary: that Symbolism was still the dominant mode of French poetry and that it would continue to grow. This, for example, was the thesis of the poet Robert de Souza, whose hortatory tract *Où Nous en sommes* appeared in 1906. And there was a grain of truth in his position: that year was to mark a resurgence of the word *Symbolism* or, rather, *neo-Symbolism.*[5] But the tide had really turned, and Symbolism was on the decline. A brief revival and a few hesitant farewells do not change this fact.

In Russia, Symbolism began to wane around 1910. In that year a new school, Futurism, published its first effort (although some might push the birth of Russian Futurism

---

3. K. Cornell, *The Post-Symbolist Period,* p. 24.

4. Verlaine was third, but he was hardly to be connected with the Symbolists. He himself had always refused the title "Symbolist," and the subsequent linking of his name with the Symbolists derived largely from his personal association with Rimbaud and from foreign critics such as Arthur Symons.

5. See M. Raymond, *From Baudelaire to Surrealism,* pp. 109 and ff.

back to 1908),[6] and in May of 1910 Ivanov and Blok published side-by-side historical analyses of Symbolism, the former's entitled "The Legacies of Symbolism" and the latter's "The Present State of Russian Symbolism." [7] *Vesy*, the revue that was the bastion of Russian Symbolism, had closed down in 1909, claiming that Symbolism's goal had been reached and the magazine no longer had a raison d'être: "We do not mean to say by this that the Symbolist movement is dead, that Symbolism has ceased to play a role as the ideological catchword of our era . . . But tomorrow it will become a different catchword, it will burn with a new flame." [8] Reacting to this statement, the young poet Nikolai Gumilëv, still a protegé of the Symbolists, replied:

> But the question of whether Symbolism need still exist as a literary school has, for the present, very little hope of being settled fully. Symbolism was founded not by the will of a single person, as was the Parnasse by the will of Leconte de Lisle, nor was it the result of a public upheaval, as was Romanticism; it appeared as the consequence of a maturing of the human spirit, proclaiming that "the world is our representation." Therefore, it can only appear outmoded when humanity rejects this thesis and rejects it not only on paper, but in its whole being. As to when that will happen, I defer judgment to the philosophers. For the present, we are unable not to be Symbolists. That is not an appeal, nor wishful thinking, I am simply certifying a fact.[9]

However much he certified at the time, the "fact" underwent a drastic revision at Gumilëv's own hands. Less than two years later, he was writing the Acmeist Manifesto, and in 1913 he proclaimed, "It is clear to the attentive reader that

6. See Vl. Markov, *The Longer Poems of Velimir Khlebnikov*, pp. 1-13.

7. Both printed in *Apollon* (May–June 1910), pp. 5-30.

8. *Vesy*, no. 12 (December 1909).

9. Nikolai Gumilëv, "Žižn' stixa," *Apollon* (April 1910), p. 14.

Symbolism has terminated its cycle of growth and is now on the decline." [10] What was on the way up was his own new school (the Acmeists), and the Futurists.

Common Trends

The ten-year span separating the wanings of the French and Russian Symbolist schools corresponds roughly to the gap between their beginnings, and the declining days of Symbolism in France and Russia show common points and common trends, just as, in their heyday, Symbolists from both countries had shown a tendency to form similar subgroups (see above, Chapter 1). Some of these trends are most important, for they helped to change the meaning of the word *Symbolism* for the new generation of poets.

One common trend apparent in the years just preceding Symbolism's decline in France and Russia was a tendency on the part of the Symbolists to fit the movement more harmoniously into their own national literatures and, in particular, to reassert the continuity between the Romantics, the Parnassians, and themselves. Symbolism was no longer viewed as a protest movement and could now conceive of itself more and more in the literary continuum. This view was first asserted in France in Emmanuel Signoret's "Première Lettre sur la poésie," published in 1896.[11] It is stated still more emphatically by Vjačeslav Ivanov in the *Apollon* article cited above, in which the author speaks of a "native Symbolist tendency" in Russian literature, manifest most directly in the works of Tjutčev, as well as in the poetry of Žukovskij, Pushkin, Boratynskij, and Lermontov.[12]

As Symbolism was seeking its own place in literary history, the Symbolists began to hew away the more "extremist" doctrines of their school's early histories. Camille Mauclair, in a paean to Jules Laforgue, attacked the outspoken statements of artistic purity set down by the Symbolists and

10. In *Apollon* (January 1913), p. 42.
11. *Mercure de France* 17 (January 1896): 29-36.
12. *Apollon* (May–June 1910), pp. 5-20.

took an indirect jibe at Mallarmé's concept of *Le Livre,* the end-product of all existence:

> Qu'est-ce que les livres, sinon des gages de ce qu'on devient, et quelle misère pernicieuse que de les prendre en eux-mêmes, de s'appauvrir pour eux, de ne sentir, de ne recueillir, de ne réfléchir, de n'aimer que pour eux! Quel dédoublement criminel, quel avilissement de soi, quel servage envers l'autrui! [13]

Francis Viélé-Griffin, writing in the same journal, made a similar attack on "l'Art pour l'Art" theorists in 1895. Citing with approval Maurice Leblond's condemnation of *la littérature artificielle* and the Des Esseintes strain in Symbolism, Viélé-Griffin concluded that these "gamineries" were now over and that Symbolism had entered a new era in aesthetics.[14] In Russia the younger poets were attacking the mystical and metaphysical orientation of the early Symbolists—Solovëv, the early Blok, Ivanov—and on this point the Futurists [15] and Acmeists concurred. As Nikolai Gumilëv, leader of the Acmeists, wrote in 1913:

> Russian Symbolism spent its mightiest efforts in the realm of the unknown. It fraternized alternately with mysticism, theosophy and occultism. Some of its searching in this direction nearly brought it to the creation of myth. And it can now rightly ask of that movement coming to replace it . . . what sort of relationship it will have to the unknowable. Well, the first thing Acmeism might reply is that the unknown, by the very meaning of the word, is impossible to become acquainted with . . . The entire beauty and sacred significance of the stars lies in the fact that they are infinitely far from the earth, and by no efforts of modern aviation will they come any closer.[16]

13. *Mercure de France* 17 (March 1896): 326.
14. *Mercure de France* 16 (October 1895): 9.
15. Markov, *Khlebnikov,* p. 4.
16. *Apollon* (January 1913), p. 44.

As some of the cherished heritage of the first Symbolists was being challenged, a subtle rewriting of literary history took place, and the reputation of the Symbolists underwent a shift at this point—one that was to change the notion of what *Symbolist* meant for the new generations in France, Russia, England, and the United States. The shift was precipitated by two new groups.

The first consisted of the so-called classical or neoclassical Symbolists. Some of these, like Henri de Régnier—whose reputation at the turn of the century was immense—were members of the original group of Symbolists; others were the survivors of the old Romanist group of Moréas (himself still quite active); [17] and still others, such as Valéry, belonged to the new generation. It was the same in Russia: on the one hand, there was Ivanov, an old Classicist, and on the other, Gumilëv, an Acmeist. In the United States the trend finds its parallel in such Classicists as T. S. Eliot.

The classical Symbolists and their followers were "classical" in several different ways: for some, like Moréas or Régnier, Classicism meant a return to the past, and they used old verse forms and reintroduced mythological subjects and motifs into their poetry; others, such as Valéry, were considered Classicists because they refuted "romantic" inspiration in favor of ordered, conscious creation (his "Introduction à la Méthode de Léonard de Vinci," printed in the August issue of the *Nouvelle Revue,* 1895, is a strong statement of this view), and argued for a formal symmetry and harmony. In Russia both classicisms were combined. The first article ever printed in the Symbolist *Apollon* was an editorial toying with the ideals of Classicism:

> Classicism, the imitation of the greatest artists of Greece and the Renaissance, if it is possible again, will only exist as a fleeting admiration, or as a protest against the formless impudence of art which has forgotten the laws of cultural succession. In truth, this

17. Cornell, Post-Symbolist Period, pp. 38, 58, 90, 97.

protest is making itself felt today in literature and in the plastic arts, and it is possibly destined to take on even sharper, more formalized dimensions.[18]

Yet, the editorial continues, art cannot return to the past, but must strive for a "new truth" in style and form. The editors' reluctant-suitor attitude toward the past is understandable in would-be innovators, yet suitors they were nonetheless. And when the journal switched from Symbolism to Acmeism, the last vestiges of the *Dekadenty* in the magazine's orientation—the pre-Raphaelite-like etchings and paintings that had adorned its pages—were judiciously dropped in favor of photographs of classical and neoclassical statues.

The *école symboliste* had shown some tendency toward Classicism since its inception, and, indeed, many poets had seen as the chief virtue of Symbolism its possibilities for asserting one or another poetic value from the past. But in the first days of the twentieth century this tendency became pronounced—partly because of the importance of Régnier in France and Russia,[19] and also through critics such as Maurras, the independent neoclassical schools,[20] and the general move to greater clarity and organization made in the name of Classicism. The so-called classical renaissance, though not a particularly Symbolist phenomenon, came to characterize Symbolism in the minds of the poets emerging in the new century.

18. *Apollon* (October 1909), p. 3.
19. Régnier's effect on the Russians is not to be underestimated. *Apollon* (no. 4, pp. 18-34) ran an unprecedented lead article on him in January 1910 (the first article in the magazine ever devoted to a single author), stating: "In the present decade Henri de Régnier belongs to the first rank of French prose-writers, just as he does in poetry. This is already a *fait accompli*, silently acknowledged by his contemporaries." The author, M. Vološin, sees Régnier as some sort of pioneer, a "neo-realist" who was able to accept symbolism but go beyond its constructedness and artificiality (pp. 26-28).
20. Décaudin, *Crise des valeurs symbolistes*, pp. 309-30.

The second big change in the meaning of Symbolism for the younger generation also involved an international group, but was centered around one man, Jules Laforgue. Laforgue had, of course, been a member of the original Symbolist school, a close friend of Gustave Kahn, and a frequenter of Mallarmé's "mardi soirs." He was praised highly by Mallarmé, Kahn, and the critic Téodor de Wyzéwa. Yet in the course of his lifetime he published only two volumes-worth of work (*Moralités légendaires* did not appear until three months after his death in 1887; his *Derniers Vers* were published in 1890). Furthermore, his thinking was too far removed from the orthodoxy of Mallarmé and his *cénacle* for him to be an accepted spokesman for the Symbolists, and he remained a peripheral member of the movement.[21] For both these reasons it was a while before Laforgue's specific contribution to the Symbolist period—broadly, the ironic stance of a *Pierrot lunaire*—came to be recognized by the generation of new poets as a Symbolist phenomenon.

Whether in fact one may associate Laforguian irony with Symbolism is hard to say, all the more so because of the difficulty of setting out Symbolist aesthetic views in even the most general terms. Laforgue certainly shared with the Symbolists an abhorrence of effusive, personal emotion in poetry: they avoided it, he mocked it. And underlying his ironic stance is the same Symbolist sense of the complexity of things perceived: where Mallarmé and the others typically make of a poem the unification and resolution of this complexity (e.g. the poem "Soupir" discussed in Chapter 3), Laforgue states it as a constant, internal dividedness in his speakers—as unending contradiction and opposition. Yet to the Symbolist love of rhetoric, Laforgue opposed anti-rhetoric—slang, the sloppy diction of the uneducated peasant, strained puns, and a recourse to rhythm and rhyme for ironic purposes. And while most Symbolist poems were

21. See Ramsey, *Jules Laforgue*, pp. 180 and ff.; 4-10. This is an excellent study of Laforgue's contribution.

a priori unable to use a dramatic or narrative construction, these are the very forms that Laforgue loved.

More basic still, the ironic stance severely limits pursuit of the Symbolist goal of mystery and strangeness. Inasmuch as Laforgue's poetry is "human, all too human," [22] its search for strangeness is inevitably focused on the character of the speaker(s). As was shown in the previous chapter, this is the strangeness of Sologub or Brjusov, not Mallarmé or Maeterlinck or Saint-Pol-Roux. To try to make an admittedly difficult distinction, it is a strangeness that requires comprehension in order to be strange, and it cannot, therefore, operate on a purely verbal level. For Laforgue's poetry constantly asserts internal paradox (which is at the heart of self-mockery), and a paradox must be comprehended on a verbal level, its meaning must be clear, before it can be paradoxical. Beyond this point, as is evident from the examples cited, strangeness may still operate; for what we comprehend on the level of verbal meaning may nonetheless remain ungrasped on other levels; we can know all about the desire for self-destruction and still never understand the speaker of *Grjaduščie Gunny.* Yet such poems cannot have the purely verbal mysteriousness of a poem by Maeterlinck or Mallarmé.

Laforgue's brand of irony was not altogether foreign to the poetry of the Symbolists. Rimbaud had gone through an ironic phase (the time of "Ce qu'on dit au poète à propos des fleurs"), as had the Verlaine of *Fêtes galantes.* More important than either of these, Tristan Corbière, one of Verlaine's original *poètes maudits,* had helped bring irony to Symbolism. However he differed from Laforgue in style and outlook,[23] Corbière was closer to him than any other poet of the Symbolist period, and the two together had represented an ironic adjunct to the main figures of the school. Yet they were, until the late 1890s, only an adjunct: the aesthetic

22. Ibid., p. 7.
23. Ibid., pp. 95-100.

gulf between the ironists and the Mallarmean Symbolists was too great to admit both.

By the 1890s, given the general shift of sensibilities, this was no longer the case. The attacks on forced diction, unified abstractions, and extreme doctrines had argued that these were not necessarily the sine qua non of Symbolist poetry. In the process, the question of what a Symbolist poet is had been changed to who the Symbolist poets were. To this last question, "Laforgue" had always been a possible answer; with the new desire for a commonplace, even colloquial diction, naturalness, and "Yankee straightforwardness," [24] he began to be acknowledged as one of the most important of the Symbolists. Mauclair's article on Laforgue, a two-part, forty-five-page elegy,[25] marked a turning point not only in the poet's reputation but in the fortunes of other Symbolist ironists. The article is an unending series of superlatives:

> Vraiment [Laforgue] c'est le moderne même, dans sa plus logique et plus pure manifestation, et nous ne pouvons pas choisir parmi nos morts une figure plus chère . . .

> Par son mélange de sensibilité aiguë et d'ironie, Laforgue, comme par son style, fut *Français et clair,* et il est absurde, injuste, déconcertant, non qu'on ait pris de lui et de ses écrits peu de soin, mais que ceux qui s'en occupèrent (hormis nous, ses amis et camarades d'art récent) ne l'aient pas vu . . .

24. The magazine *L'Ermitage* had been instrumental in an American renaissance, publishing—among others—Whitman and Mark Twain. Whitman's *Leaves of Grass* was translated in full in 1908, and his poetry had an important effect on several poets at the turn of the century. (Marcel Raymond discusses Whitman in terms of the Naturists and Unanimists; see his *Baudelaire to Surrealism,* pp. 61, 191, and ff.)

25. *Mercure de France* 17 (March 1896): 302-27.

WAYNESBURG COLLEGE LIBRARY
WAYNESBURG, PA.

Les *Moralités Légendaires* demeurent un monument singulier et unique dans notre littérature. Je n'y connais point d'analogue . . .

. . . Je n'ai, pour dire "génie" et "chef d'œuvre" de quoi que ce soit en art, aucune raison plus sincère, plus motivée et plus sérieuse que Jules Laforgue.

As Laforgue's reputation grew,[26] so did the ironic current of the Symbolist period. In France it gained a number of new admirers, including Gide, and disciples such as L.-P. Fargue and Alain-Fournier. In Russia, Sologub underwent a revival, and his old saw: "Two eternal truths, two ways of knowledge, are given to man: one is lyrical—it denies and destroys the world; the other is ironical—it accepts the world to the end," was being memorized by schoolboys.[27] Even Blok, though too thoroughly earnest to become an ironist, had undergone a change and, by 1910, was writing poems of self-mocking melancholy. In the United States, Laforgue was having a profound effect on Eliot and Pound,[28] and Hart Crane was translating three of the "Locutions des Pierrots." Eliot, with Arthur Symons and the critic James Huneker, was the chief interpreter of French Symbolism to the English-speaking world—so that, through him, Laforgue and Corbière were translated into two of the most important figures of the Symbolist school. In an oft-quoted remark, Eliot acknowledged that the reading of Laforgue, Rimbaud, Verlaine, and Corbière had "affected the course of my life." [29] And in so doing, it had brought the ironic Symbolists to the attention of American poets.

26. See Ramsey, *Jules Laforgue,* pp. 178 and ff.

27. See Slonim, *Modern Russian Literature,* p. 184.

28. See Ramsey, pp. 178 and ff. and Taupin, *l'Influence du symbolisme français.*

29. First written in a 1930 review of Peter Quennell's *Baudelaire and the Symbolists.* Edmund Wilson later quoted him in *Axel's Castle,* p. 93: "The form in which I began to write, in 1908 or 1909, was directly drawn from the study of Laforgue together with the later Elizabethan drama."

Thus, by the end of World War I a major shift had taken place in aesthetics. Poets emerging at this time were subject to a variety of influences—influences that were present not only in France but in Russia and the United States as well. Among these were the various new schools, many of which have been mentioned in passing in the previous section, and the most striking of which were, perhaps, the recent "defiance" movements of Futurism in Russia and Dada in Western Europe.[30] More important still was the influence of the now-waning Symbolism; it was, of course, not quite the Symbolism that the Symbolists themselves had known, nor the Symbolism we know today.[31] The young poets of the time were rather ambivalent in their attitude toward the Symbolists. Many of the aesthetic questions that had been so important to the Symbolists were simply irrelevant now. The whole issue of anti-Positivism and alienation from scientific methods of inquiry must have appeared somewhat dated in the Machine Age; Nietzsche was considered a far more important thinker than Schopenhauer or Hegel; the Parnassians were no longer perceived as an aesthetic challenge or threat; and any attempt to isolate poetry from social, moral, or (in the extreme) temporal questions was to be viewed with suspicion after two revolutions in Russia and a World War. Yet Symbolism was still unquestionably the biggest thing to happen in poetry since Romanticism. If its aesthetics were no longer tenable, much very beautiful po-

30. I mention these two movements in the same breath not because they are doctrinally similar (they are not), but because they shared a desire to outrage, which, if not a literary doctrine, is at least an attitude about literature that is communicated to other writers. The outrageous excesses of Dada are well-known; for some of Futurism's outrages, starting with the manifesto *Poščeščina obščestvennomu vkusu* [A Slap in the Face of Public Taste], see Markov, *Khlebnikov*, pp. 9 and ff.

31. The latter because Mallarmé's aesthetics were not well understood, Rimbaud was still too much the *enfant terrible* revered by Breton et al., and Valéry and Claudel had not yet achieved their real prominence.

etry had already been written in its name, and it was difficult to reject all this because of differences in philosophical and aesthetic outlook. Furthermore, in so heterogeneous a movement, there were subgroups and currents (such as neoclassicism and irony) which retained an appeal to young poets.

To illustrate the new generation's attitudes, I have selected three "heirs of Symbolism" from three countries in which the impact of Symbolism on post-Symbolist poets was particularly important: France, Russia, and the United States.[32] These poets, Jules Supervielle, Osip Mandel'štam, and Hart Crane, share many common traits. None of the three may be considered the single, outstanding poet of his generation,[33] but all were unquestionably prominent poets of their generation. Moreover, the work of each of them well illustrates how Symbolism has perpetuated itself in modern poetry, and what sorts of problems this perpetuation has raised.

Jules Supervielle was born in 1884; he was a day shy of seven years old when Osip Mandel'štam was born and a little over fifteen at Hart Crane's birth. All three poets started writing at an early age: Supervielle and Crane both published their first poems at the age of sixteen, Mandel'štam at the age of nineteen. These dates of first publication—1900, 1910, and 1916 respectively—roughly correspond to the "moment of waning" of Symbolism in the three countries represented.[34] In other words, as each was starting out, Sym-

32. Symbolism did not play a particularly crucial part in postwar England: Auden, Spender, or Thomas may have been influenced by it, but not greatly so, and Yeats could not be considered an "heir," for he belonged to the Symbolist generation. For this reason I have not continued the discussion of English poetry in this section.

33. It is difficult to think of this generation as having a "dominant figure" in any of the countries involved, although this may be due to our lack of perspective; certainly, there was no one who "dominated" in the way Hugo or even Mallarmé had some years earlier. Rather, one finds three or four poets of equal importance in each country: Apollinaire, Claudel, Valéry, Supervielle, Eluard; Xlebnikov, Majakovskij, Mandel'štam, Pasternak, Axmatova; Eliot, Pound, Stevens, Crane.

34. In the United States, of course, it is impossible to speak of a "waning" at all; the year 1916 is significant in that it was about this

bolism already had its new found reputation for both classicism and irony, and had been subjected to a certain amount of critical inquiry as well.

Both Crane and Supervielle fell under the influence of Laforgue, although neither ended up adopting the ironist aesthetic of Laforgue's verse. For Supervielle the influence was almost inevitable: biographical similarities—starting with their common, exiled birthplace, Montevideo—must have attracted him to Laforgue from the outset.[35] Indeed, in a 1919 poem he lavishly addresses Laforgue as his "furtif nourricier":

> Loin de ta chère Ombre importune
> Ah! Fais-moi une
> Petite place dans la Lune!

Crane came to Laforgue by an indirect route—the imitative Laforguian verse of Eliot and Pound. Although, of course, Laforgue's effect on Crane was not nearly so profound, Crane was still deeply attracted to him, as may be seen in his translations of the Laforgue's "Locutions" (undertaken despite Crane's feeble knowledge of French), in the poem "Chaplinesque," and in sections of "Faustus and Helen": "And you may fall downstairs with me / With perfect grace and equanimity." Sometimes, as here, Crane writes "pure Laforgue," while elsewhere in the poem the mediation of Eliot is clearly felt:

> O, I have known metallic paradises
> Where cuckoos clucked to finches
> Above the deft catastrophes of drums.
> While titters hailed the groans of death
> Beneath gyrating awnings I have seen

---

time that Eliot began to publish imitations of Laforgue and Corbière for the American public. *Prufrock* was printed in England in 1917 and reissued in the United States in 1920.

35. The third famous Montevidean of this period was Isidore Ducasse, "le comte de Lautréamont."

> The incunabula of the divine grotesque.
> The music has a reassuring way.

Despite such evidence, however, it must be said that the importance of Laforgue for Supervielle and Crane was a symptom of the times; for neither was he a lasting influence.[36]

Mandel'štam was apparently unaffected by Laforgue and the French ironists, but he was clearly impressed with Annenskij and Sologub, both of whom represented strands of Laforguian thought in Russian verse. In Annenskij he saw "the first student of psychological pungency in the new Russian lyric," while he characterized Sologub as "having purged [the nineteenth-century lyric] of its trash-heap emotionalism and tinged it with an original, erotic mythos." [37] Moreover, it was inevitable that he should be influenced by the neoclassical Symbolists as well. Since as a young man Mandel'štam was one of the original Acmeists, Gumilëv's hard-line Classicism no doubt played an important role in shaping his views. However, like Gumilëv, he had a difficult time reconciling a literary retrogression with the necessity for embracing one's own times. In an early essay, Mandel'štam finds a way out in asserting the contemporaneity of all literature for the emerging poet—or, more precisely, its potential contemporaneity:

> It often happens that you hear someone say, "That's fine, but it's from a day long past." But I say that past day

36. See Ramsey, *Jules Laforgue,* pp. 178-91, 213-22. Having cited Supervielle's "furtif nourricier" poem, Ramsey adds: "One of the most honest of poets, anxious to escape a dominion he was the readiest to admit, Supervielle was never possessed by Laforgue to the same degree as T. S. Eliot was" (p. 185). Similarly, "No doubt it would be difficult to find two poets presenting greater temperamental, environmental, intellectual differences [than Crane and Laforgue] . . . Differences recognized, it becomes all the more significant that Crane, in a word, *liked* Laforgue, and that he imitated and translated him in the decisive years when his own dissimilar style was being formed" (pp. 214-15).

37. Osip Mandel'štam, *Sobranie Sočinenij,* 2 : 386.

has not yet been born. It has not really existed. I want
some Ovid, Pushkin and Catullus anew, and won't be
satisfied with the historic Ovid, Pushkin or Catullus.

The essay adds, "Revolution in art inevitably leads to classicism." [38] While Crane's neoclassicism was somewhat less
exuberant,[39] not even for Mandel'štam was it a fundamental
influence: it was, like Laforguian irony, important for the
new generation as a passively experienced phenomenon, and
was simply part of what literature meant in the early twentieth century.

Given the pattern of influences external or peripheral to
the "traditional" Symbolist aesthetic, it would appear that
little of that aesthetic had survived. Certainly, its heirs, the
Supervielle-Mandel'štam-Crane generation, no longer shared
many of its preoccupations: anti-Positivism, the German
idealistic thinkers, the inroads of science and technology on
the modern world. Indeed, on the last point they are quite
specific. Supervielle holds up the scientist as a model for
poets in his methodical pursuit of wisdom; [40] Crane, approaching the question in the broader context of a poet's
place in the modern world, adds:

The function of poetry in a Machine Age is identical
to its function in any other age; and its capacities for
presenting the most complete synthesis of human values
remain essentially immune from any of the so-called
inroads of science . . . For unless poetry can absorb
the machine, i.e. *acclimatize* it as naturally and casually
as trees, cattle, galleons, castles and all other human

38. "Slovo i Kul'tura," in *Sobranie Sočinenij*, 2 : 266.
39. It comes mostly through Eliot (whose criticism Crane much
admired)—an important point—for in Eliot the identification of Symbolism and neoclassicism was maintained. See Crane's letter to Solomon Grunberg (September 30, 1930), in *The Letters of Hart Crane*,
ed. Brom Weber p. 356.
40. *Naissances*, p. 67.

associations of the past, then poetry has failed of its full contemporary function.[41]

Behind this notion stands an even more basic principle: a disbelief in the arguments for literary progress or evolution, a refusal to conceive of this as a New Age,[42] and an acceptance of this world in this point of time as the "given" from which poetry is to arise. Crane and Mandel'štam elaborate different aspects of this idea:

> The deliberate program, then, of a "break" with the past or tradition seems to me to be a sentimental fallacy . . . I put no particular value on the simple objective of "modernity." The element of the temporal location of an artist's creation is of very secondary importance; it can be left to the impressionist or historian just as well.[43]

> The theory of progress in literature is the rankest, the most repulsive aspect of scholastic ignorance. Literary forms change, and some forms take the place of others. But each change, each such acquisition is accompanied by a loss. There can be nothing "better," no progress in literature, simply because literature is not a machine, nor is there any "finish-line" which one must get to before the others.[44]

But perhaps the most revealing question in regard to the rift between the Symbolists and their heirs is that of the poet's relation to his reader. For the Symbolists the question was raised in terms of Symbolist "obscurity" and "poetry for the initiated," and the Symbolists' answer was infamous in its own time: "Si un être d'une intelligence moyenne, et

---

41. "Modern Poetry," reprinted in *Complete Poems and Selected Letters and Prose of Hart Crane*, ed. Brom Weber, pp. 261–62.

42. Cf. Symbolism's conception of the turn of the century, the Second Coming, and the "New Dawn" discussed in Chap. 1.

43. Crane, "General Aims and Theories," in *Complete Poems*, p. 218.

44. Mandel'štam, "O prirode slova," in *Sobranie Sočinenij*, 2 : 285–86.

d'une préparation littéraire insuffisante, ouvre par hasard un
livre ainsi fait et prétend en jouir, il y a malentendu, il faut
remettre les choses à leur place." [45] The book "ainsi fait"
was a book of good poetry, in which "there must always be
enigma." For the Symbolists the question of the reader *became* the question of mysteriousness and evocativeness; and
their answer, as has been seen, postulated either no audience
("Pure Art"), an uncomprehending audience, or one "initiated" into the aesthetics of enigma.

For the new generation the role of the reader assumes
more importance, perhaps because of—or in sympathy with
—the criticism of Symbolism's disregard for the reader,
which began to appear in the late 1890s. The new poets
were no longer interested in proclaiming poetry's independence of the reader, but rather in discovering what demands
could be placed on him. "This question," Hart Crane wrote
in a famous letter to Harriet Monroe, "is more important to
me than it perhaps ought to be; but as long as poetry is
written, an audience, however small, is implied, and there
remains the question of an active or inactive imagination as
its characteristic." [46] What these poets criticized in their
predecessors was a failure to consider this audience; they
were poets who "se laissent aller au seul plaisir de se
délivrer et ne s'inquiètent nullement de la beauté du poème.
Ou, pour me servir d'une autre image, ils remplissent leur
verre à ras bord et oublient de vous servir, vous, lecteur." [47]
Mandel'štam brings up the question when he contrasts
Sologub and Bal'mont: "Sologub, in the various ways he
relates to the reader, is a most interesting antipode to
Bal'mont. Several qualities lacking in Bal'mont are found
in abundance in Sologub: specifically, a love and respect for
his interlocutor." [48] Inevitably, if the reader were to be con-

45. Mallarmé's response to Jules Huret's *Enquête*, reprinted in the
former's *Œuvres complètes*, pp. 866–72.

46. *Complete Poems*, p. 238.

47. Supervielle, *Naissances*, p. 61.

48. "O Sobesednike" [On the Interlocutor], *Sobranie Sočinenij*,
2 : 282.

sidered, the basic question of the goal of strangeness and mysteriousness had to be raised. Mandel'šam's essay "On the Interlocutor" argues that the poet writes, not for his immediate audience, but for an "interlocutor" who is always remote from the poet. It is from the "distance of separation" (*rasstojanie razluki*) that the "dialogue" (*dialoga*) between poet and reader can become a two-way operation:

> The logic is unimpeachable. If I know the person with whom I am speaking, I know in advance how he is to relate to what I am saying—whatever I may say—and, consequently, I have no chance to be amazed at his amazement, to rejoice in his joy, to come to love his love. The distance of separation erases the familiar traits of a person. Only then does there arise in me a desire to say those important things which I could not have said when I held sway over his attitude in its full and present plenitude. This observation might well be formulated thus: the value of our communicating is indirectly proportional to our real knowledge of the interlocutor and directly proportional to our own attempt to gain his interest.[49]

In the poet's attempt to gain the reader's interest across this distance, strangeness may be a possible recourse; mystery may survive, in Mandel'štam's view, so long as it attracts. It is not, however, asserted as a value or as an essence of poetry, nor is incomprehension accountable in such a view. Supervielle states it more emphatically:

> Le poète dispose de deux pédales, la claire lui permet d'aller jusqu'à la transparence, l'obscure jusqu'à l'opacité. Je crois n'avoir que rarement appuyé sur la pedale obscure. . . . Je n'ai guère connu la peur de la banalité qui hante la plupart des écrivains mais bien plutôt celle de l'incompréhension et de la singularité. N'écrivant pas pour des spécialistes du

mystère j'ai toujours souffert quand une personne sensible ne comprenait pas un de mes poèmes.[50]

Supervielle, in the brief bits of criticism available to us, thus questions some of the Symbolists' most basic principles. To Mallarmé's injunction against the functions of prose, "narrer, enseigner, même décrire," he answers, "le conteur surveille en moi le poète."[51] For Mandel'štam, Symbolism in Russia is become "pseudo-symbolism," the doctrine of correspondences an "awful square-dance, everything bowing to everything else,"[52] and he can see no need "to entertain oneself with a stroll into the 'forest of symbols.' "[53] Symbolism for Crane was Laforgue and Rimbaud, not Mallarmé and the literary *cénacles* of the 1880s:

> There always remains the cult of "words," elegancies, elaborations, to exhibit with a certain amount of pride to an "inner circle" of literary intimates. But this is, to me, rivaled by numerous other forms of social accomplishment which might, if attained, provide as mild and seductive recognitions.[54]

For the same "cult of 'words,' " Supervielle adds:

> Malgré les merveilleux exemples de certains poètes qui transforment les mots en objets précieux, j'écris souvent sans penser aux mots, je m'efforce même d'oublier leur existence pour cerner de plus étroitement ma pensée.[55]

And with that, it would seem that the last remnants of what has been called the "Symbolist aesthetic" had been cast aside.

50. *Naissances*, pp. 60-61.
51. Ibid., p. 62.
52. Literally, "strašnyj kontredans sootvetstvij."
53. *Sobranie Sočinenij*, 2 : 365.
54. Letter to Waldo Frank, June 20, 1926; in his *Complete Poems*, p. 232.
55. *Naissances*, p. 63.

6.   Three Modern Poems

"Modernism" is a curious phenomenon, a disunified flow of writing that began in the early part of this century and is still going strong. Its relationship to Symbolism is more complex than some of its early representatives—Supervielle, Crane, and Mandel'štam are not alone—allowed for in their rejection of Symbolist values. For, anyone familiar with the poetry of these or other Moderns must nowadays read their refutation of the Symbolists' stance with some amusement, since there is one undeniable fact about a great deal of Modernist writing: it is so much *like* the poetry of Mallarmé and Maeterlinck, Roux and Rimbaud. For all the stated differences in aesthetic aims, there is an unmistakable resemblance between the poetry of these two generations— a resemblance that would argue that the "heritage of Symbolism" was not for the new poets a minor part of their literary backgrounds much less the object of poetic revolt —but the stylistic basis of their own writing.

While the resemblance cannot be "proven" by anything short of a full reading of the poetry of this new generation, it can be illustrated in any number of citations. For it is not difficult to find, among these new poets, the same Symbolist taste for mystery and strangeness:

> Sous un azur très ancien
> Cachant de célestes patries
> Les roses ceignant des palmiers
> Tendent vers la Rose infinie.
>
> Entre des statues brahmaniques
> Aux sourires envahisseurs
> La haute terrasse d'honneur
> Cède à sa grande nostalgie
>
> Et d'obsédantes pyramides
> Lèvent un doigt bleui de ciel
> Vers quelque but essentiel
> Par delà l'aérien vide.

Dans l'heure mille et millénaire
Qui trempe au fond des temps secrets
Pour qui ces roses et ces pierres
Qui n'ont jamais désespéré? ¹

The resemblance is not merely a picking-up of Symbolist
mannerisms, although, as this poem of Supervielle's illustrates, such mannerisms as the Symbolists had were not lost
on the younger generation.² Rather, it is a more basic kin-
ship. What Supervielle, Mandel'štam, and Crane had inherited were the very structures evolved by the Symbolists
to meet their goal of strangeness: the use of incomplete
reference and implied iconographic significance in the single-
image or string-of-images constructions seen in Chapter 4.
The three poems in the present chapter will recapitulate
these structures and make the inheritance somewhat clearer.
The following is Mandel'štam's "Sisters":

Сестры — тяжесть и нежность — одинаковы ваши
приметы.
Медуницы и осы тяжелую розу сосут.
Человек умирает, песок остывает согретый,
И вчерашнее солнце на черных носилках несут.

Ах, тяжелые соты и нежные сети
Легче камень поднять, чем имя твое повторить!
У меня остается одна забота на свете:
Золотая забота, как времени бремя избыть.

Словно темную воду я пью помутившийся воздух.
Время вспахано плугом, и роза землею была.
В медленном водовороте тяжелые нежные розы,
Розы тяжесть и нежность в двойные венки заплела.³

1. Supervielle, "Regret de l'Asie en Amérique," *Gravitations* p. 49.
2. I am referring to usages such as "un azur très ancien," "la Rose
infinie," "par delà l'aérien vide"—phrases which are so reminiscent of
Mallarmé's first contributions to *Le Parnasse Contemporain*.
3.
You Sisters, heaviness and tenderness, share the same traits.
Honeybees and wasps are suckled by one heavy rose. Man dies,

Mandel'štam's poem is, like Roux's "Liminaire," built around the string-of-images construction, and the salvageable sense of continuity is again dependent on the reader's ability to link vague associations clinging to the different images into a single whole.[4] This is a love-poem, although it may not be immediately apparent to the reader, particularly in translation. *Nežnost'* ("tenderness") is almost a synonym in Russian for love, and "rose," in the lexical iconography of Russian, is even more closely associated with love than in English. These two facts, along with two mysterious "hints" (the "thy" in line 6 and an unexplained feminine verb form in the last line), seem to indicate that the speaker's love for a woman is the subject of this lyric.

The poem begins with a bold, paradoxical assertion: that heaviness and tenderness are "sisters," that they share the same traits. Phonetically, Mandel'štam has a point: *tjažest'* and *nežnost'*, two feminine nouns, are indeed similar to the ear. Yet the words are nearly opposite in meaning: *tjažest'* means heaviness, gravity (the scientific term), weight, while *nežnost'* is tenderness, delicacy, almost lightness. The next line attempts to illustrate or justify the initial assertion, al-

---

the warm sands cool, and yesterday's sun is borne by on a black stretcher.

Oh, the heavy honeycombs and tender nets, it is easier to lift up a rock than to repeat thy name! I've one care left in the world: a golden care, how to shake off the burden of time.

I drink in the stirred-up air as if it were dark water. Time is upturned by a plow, and the rose once was earth. In the slow-turning whirlpool the heavy tender roses, the Rose's heaviness and tenderness she has woven into two-fold garlands.
                                        —*Sobranie Sočinenij*, 1 : 76-77

4. As with Roux's poem (see p. 46, n. 3), I must again apologize for the translation—and for the same reason. Like Roux, Mandel'štam succeeds in linking the most disparate phrases through sound association, and almost every line is pulled together by an internal rhyme or a pattern of alliteration or assonance: to cite some of the more obvious examples, "umiraet . . . ostivaet," "soti . . . seti," "vodu . . . vozdux."

though the sense is not entirely clear. The heavy, solid honey-bee and the light, aerial wasp suck from the same rose, which is itself a "heavy" rose. Thus these two polarized creatures—the bee associated with *tjažest'*, the wasp with *nežnost'*—are joined in the rose, as sisters of the same mother. But the rose itself, normally associated with *nežnost'*, is here emblematic of the same fusion by being described as *tjažëluju* (heavy). The sense of a parallelism is strong, even if the exact rationale is not initially apparent to the reader. The first two lines are telling us, in various ways, that heaviness and tenderness are joined, and this assertion becomes the poem's theme.

The third and fourth lines are about time—more specifically, the cyclical, on-going aspect of time: a man lives, a man dies, the sun rises, the sun sets, the sands are heated by the sun, the sands cool. The actual order of these three cycles in the sentence (man, sands, sun) is climactic. The most trivial illustration of cyclical time is a man's life (the human); then comes the sand (the terrestrial); and, finally, the sun (intersteller space). That man should be the least important figure in the sentence gives the impression of tremendous magnitude. At the same time, the image of the black stretcher—which the reader may tentatively associate with night, the blackness of space, and death—gives this vision of cyclical time a somewhat morbid cast.

The first stanza, then, presents two seemingly unrelated assertions: that heaviness and tenderness are akin to one another, and that the processes of time are cold, dark, and deadly. Again, as in Roux's "Liminaire," meaning arises from fragmentation. Thus it is only after the second line has failed to convey any meaning via the normal referential process, after *medunicy* (honeybees) and *osy* (wasps) have failed to yield any standard, iconographical significance, that the reader, with no small uncertainty, establishes a parallel with the first line.

The second stanza is similar to the first in that its two initial lines are devoted to the heaviness-tenderness theme, while the last two return to the question of time. "Oh, the heavy honeycombs and the tender nets" is similar to the bees-and-wasps image of line 2, in that the poet sends a common form (a network) through the paradigm of heaviness and tenderness. The next line is based on a pun. *Legče,* while its sense here is "easier, less difficult," literally means "lighter" and is the lexical opposite of *tjaželee,* "more difficult, heavier." "Thy name," on the other hand, the reader is inclined to consider as a reference to someone or something loved by the poet, something in the *nežnost'* camp.[5] With the play on *legče,* then, the line sounds paradoxical; its sense is: "It is lighter to lift up something heavy than to repeat something tender (light)." From this assertion the speaker moves, just as abruptly as before, to the question of time: "I've one care left in the world—a golden care, how to shake off the burden of time." His new statement, perhaps the most immediately accessible lines in the poem, sets escape from the cycle of sunrise and sunset, birth and death, as his sole remaining task on earth. In linking the two themes for a second time and without transition, Mandel'štam seems to imply a basic interrelationship, but its nature is not known to the reader.

The third stanza attempts the fusion of heaviness and tenderness approached in the previous two, as well as a joining of the heaviness-tenderness and time themes. "Dark water" and "stirred-up air" represent the same heaviness-tenderness (or, here, lightness) dichotomy. The sound similarity, *vodu* (water) and *vozdux* (air), the fact that one thinks of the verb *mutit'* (stir up) as being more readily applicable to liquid than to air, and the fact that the speaker "drinks" the air, not the water—all these argue for the same fusion as was seen in the two previous stanzas. It is, by virtue of the illustrating substances, the largest, most universal fusion possible: air and water, *nežnost' and tjažest'.* In the

5. There is no other second-person singular reference in the poem, nor is there a word to which "thy" might possibly refer; it is, therefore, an immediate and unresolvable source of incomprehension.

poem this identification upsets everything, merging all the disparate elements of the poem's world: "Time is upturned by a plow, and the rose once was earth." In this new, swirling reality, all things are fused, and the source of their fusion is the unknown feminine subject of the verb *zaplela*—thou, or love, or something else, the reader cannot know. What he does know is that this feminine subject has "woven twofold garlands," i.e. has brought together all the components of the poem, all the flashing images of heaviness and tenderness. Furthermore, the reader may come to feel that it is this very fusion which will lift the speaker "out of the burden of time" and into a new way of being.

The different ways in which the line—"Time is up-turned by a plow, and the rose once was earth"—is meaningful make it a model of the old Symbolist method, but heightened to a rare degree. The aspect of time that is significant for the sentence is its continuity, which is now perceived as discontinued ("up-turned by a plow").[6] Conversely, the most meaningful aspect of "rose" is its discreteness, its fine, delicate singleness in time and space, which is now perceived as equally lost, in view of its emergence from the continuity of earth. The fabric of the rose is the soil. The two halves of the sentence thus mirror each other, the one creating gaps where none are perceived, the other annihilating discreteness into continuity. Time is a common term in both halves: in the first it is the subject, and in the second, the unnamed agent through which the identification of rose with earth is possible. The rose is earth through history, through the time of its genesis. But rose is also a common term: in the second half, it is the subject, and in the first, an agent—the rose of love, which has caused the speaker to perceive the upturning of time. Finally, the two halves reveal a chiasmus of associations. For normally, plow and earth belong together as actor and acted-upon; and in the rationale of the poem, rose and time also belong together, and in the same relationship.

6. The phrase itself is an "irreconcilable union" in which *plow* becomes a mysterious, incomplete allusion.

In its structure the poem resembles the "string-of-images" type discussed in Chapter 4 and epitomized in a poem such as Roux's "Liminaire." Like Roux, Mandel'štam confronts the reader with an almost overwhelming flow of disjointed images. Certain aspects of it are equally reminiscent of Mallarmé's "Soupir": the grammatical ambiguities, the crossruffing of traits and characteristics between two subjects, and the process of fusion central to both poems. With both poets Mandel'štam shares the procedure of frequent parallelisms of meaning and sound, in order to unify the poem. And with most of the Symbolists Mandel'štam shares that commitment to the techniques of strangeness so basic to their poetry. In addition to the glaring mysteries of Mandel'štam's poem (Who is the "thou"? What is the subject of *zaplela?*), many of the parallelisms stated categorically in my explication are really only dimly perceived; the references of the poem cannot be "understood" in most cases. What is accessible is a participation in the synthesis that the poem attempts, a participation that is independent of "comprehension" as we normally think of it.

Hart Crane has long been connected with the Symbolists, although the Symbolist to whom he is often linked, Laforgue, is not particularly relevant to most of his work. Carl Sandburg was closer to the truth when he called Crane "the Cleveland Rimbaud"; the comparison is fitting not only from the standpoint of biography,[7] but also of style.[8] Thus the

7. The biographical similarities of Crane and Rimbaud are strong; early family difficulties, flight to the life of a Bohemian "revolté," homosexuality, and poetic careers that were cut short—Rimbaud's by Africa, Crane's by suicide.

8. Not surprisingly, much of Crane's mature poetry also resembles that of Mallarmé or Roux in its density of allusion, and such poems as "At Melville's Tomb" have a particularly Mallarmean air about them. (See Crane's famous letter to Harriet Monroe, on the latter poem, reprinted in his *Complete Poems,* pp. 234-40.) The very title of the poem suggests a translation of the French formula "Le tombeau de. . . ," the equivalent of "In Memory of. . . ." Perhaps Crane was thinking of Mallarmé's "Le Tombeau d'Edgar Poe" or "Le Tombeau de Charles Baudelaire."

following poem, "Black Tambourine," bears a close structural relationship to Rimbaud's "Le loup criait . . .":

The interests of a black man in a cellar
Mark tardy judgment on the world's closed door
Gnats toss in the shadow of a bottle,
And a roach spans a crevice in the floor.

Aesop, driven to pondering, found
Heaven with the tortoise and the hare;
Fox brush and sow ear top his grave
And mingling incantations on the air.

The black man, forlorn in the cellar,
Wanders in some mid-kingdom, dark, that lies
Between his tambourine, stuck on the wall,
And, in Africa, a carcass quick with flies.[9]

Like Rimbaud's poem, "Black Tambourine" relies largely on abrupt shifts in diction and tone to imply parallelisms and restatements. For it is a poem about "being between," trapped in a midway existence without escape—an idea that is stated several times in different images. If the explicit subject is the lot of "a black man in a cellar," he represents more than the American Negro in the early twentieth century: he is a model of "being between" in any form, and it is the universality of this state which is the poem's real concern.[10]

The first stanza sets out the black man's situation—the dingy basement surroundings that contain his life. The gnats around the bottle may be an added suggestion of his meager circumstances: his only source of light is a candle stuck in an old beer-bottle. This is a life we have heard about, and the world's insensitivity to it stands waiting for judgment—

9. Crane, *Complete Poems*, p. 4.
10. The suggestion that the poem is a statement of the poet's own "mid-kingdom," set forth in L. S. Dembo, *Hart Crane's Sanskrit Charge*, p. 40, and in R. W. B. Lewis, *The Poetry of Hart Crane*, p. 26, is really too limiting. The poem is about the state of "mid-kingdom" as a fact of human existence.

tardy judgment, for it will be of no avail to the black man already marked by his in-between state.

The relation of Aesop to the black man is not immediately clear. Some commentators [11] suggest that the fact that Aesop was himself a slave is the relevant association; but if this overtone exists, it must not be overemphasized, for the tale of the tortoise and the hare is much more important to the poem than the character of Aesop himself. We must remind ourselves, in this post-Disney age, what the story originally was: an early Greek attempt at finding an answer to the mathematical problem of limits. The "heaven" that Aesop finds in this problem is the heaven of mathematical thought, abstract contemplation in which the flesh-and-blood animals become symbols of different velocities, or of moral qualities. And what has become of this Aesop, the ponderer?

> Fox brush and sow ear top his grave
> And mingling incantations on the air.

The first two stanzas thus present two abrupt shifts: from the black man's cellar to Aesop the thinker, and from Aesop to Aesop's grave. The abruptness of both shifts implies the reader can "understand" the transition (Rimbaud's technique in "Le loup criait . . ."), and yet the relationships are only vaguely sensed, for they are quite complex. Clearly, the second shift (from Aesop to the grave) carries a strong notion of a degeneration. From Aesop's animals, the allegorical hare and tortoise, we move back to "real" creatures, fox and sow—creatures that have the same reality as the gnats and roach from which we have just come. The implication, then, is that the grave of Aesop and the cellar of the black man exist on the same level—both of them, spiritually as well as physically, six feet under.

What, though, is the significance of fox brush and sow ear? The mastery of this line comes straight from Symbolist technique. To the American ear these two terms sound a little like dialect names for wild plants (they are not), so

11. Lewis, p. 28, and Samuel Hazo, *Hart Crane*, p. 26.

that these severed anatomical parts are apt to seem like a kind of pagan flower-offering on the grave of the dead thinker. If they are not that, then to what custom or symbolic meaning might they refer? Certainly, one strong association is that of folk medicine: fox brush ($=$ fox tail) and sow ear might well come from the same witch doctor's kit that contains bats' wings, spider webs, and wolf's toe. This association is supported by the "mingling incantations" in the next line. And if the distinction of real versus allegorical creatures links "fox" and "sow" to "gnats" and "roach," then the association of black magic with the black man and his cellar is all the stronger. For Aesop the implications are clear. In death he is returned from the certainty of allegorical hares and tortoises to the mysterious reality that fox brush and sow ear evoke.

But the black man, back in his cellar, does not live wholly in either world. Both the tambourine and the "carcass quick with flies" are clichés of a Negro's existence. (The carcass, an apparent reference to some unknown story or symbolic value, is on the same level as fox brush, sow ear, and mingling incantations; it "means" primitive, repugnant, wholly foreign.) The black man's mid-kingdom lies between these two clichés, between the Aesop-like certainty of a social role and the magical, African reality of a carcass quick with flies. In his own world he has a little of both: the tambourine on the wall, the insects on the floor. And yet, unable to believe either extreme, the black man wanders in an intermediate state of consciousness—a mid-kingdom that exists between two identifiable quantities.

To the extent that the poem is talking about a sociological problem, its subject is the American Negro in the twentieth century. His society's own solutions to the problem—"in due time" or "perseverance and hard work"—is ironically echoed in the allusion to the allegorical hare and tortoise. But the poem is clearly larger than that. Like the black man, many people come to doubt the fable-like world of social roles, even though they appear to live by them; yet it is their

world, and they cannot exist in the animal reality at the
poem's other extreme. Such people have a mid-kingdom of
their own, a mixture of Aesop living and Aesop dead.
Stripped of its sociological implications, the poem is about this
unnameable semiconscious state, about men who have
neither allegorical hares and tortoises nor fox brush and sow
ear.

The subject of Supervielle's poem "Mouvement" is a gesture, the turning of a horse's head to look at some unidenti-
fied thing or happening:

> Ce cheval qui tourna la tête
> Vit ce que nul n'a jamais vu
> Puis il continua de paître
> A l'ombre des eucalyptus.
>
> Ce n'était ni homme ni arbre
> Ce n'était pas une jument
> Ni même un souvenir de vent
> Qui s'exerçait sur du feuillage.
>
> C'était ce qu'un autre cheval,
> Vingt mille siècles avant lui,
> Ayant soudain tourné la tête
> Aperçut à cette heure-ci.
>
> Et ce que nul ne reverra,
> Homme, cheval, poisson, insecte,
> Jusqu'à ce que le sol ne soit
> Que le reste d'une statuë
> Sans bras, sans jambes et sans tête.[12]

The dominance of this single, mysterious movement in the
poem is reminiscent of the singleness of Zinaida Gippius's
"Hubbub" or Mallarmé's "Soupir." Like the latter, "Mouve-
ment" is concerned with an act of unification, with two ges-
tures which come together, and a perception of this unification resolves the poem while its mystery persists.

12. Supervielle, *Gravitations*, p. 113.

As with many Symbolist poems, the immediate mystery, a thing perceived, is connected to the mystery of the perceiver; however, in this case the perceiver is not the speaker of the poem but "ce cheval." The thing he sees is not a source of astonishment; he goes back to grazing. An insignificant turn of the head to witness an insignificant sight—this is the subject of the poem. The eucalyptus trees of the first stanza, the first "detail" in the poem, remove most readers from the scene. Since it is an exotic setting, there is a certain dissonance between the landscape and the immediacy the "ce" would imply.

The second stanza is a witty catalogue of negatives, a kind of Ciceronean *praetereo*. In *not* telling the reader, Supervielle only heightens the mystery of the things perceived. "Un souvenir de vent / Qui s'exercait sur du feuillage" is a mild use of "incompatible union." As the last item on the list, this superlative of inconspicuousness seems to imply that the thing seen by the horse was still fainter and less noticeable. Why, then, is it so important? The third stanza sounds at first as if it will supply an answer, but it too ends in mystery. Indeed, its final line presents a new source of strangeness. "Saw at this very hour" is a grammatical impossibility (a peculiarly Mallarmean form of incompatible union), and its effect is to call into question the whole notion of time: a different horse, twenty thousand years earlier, and yet the same movement, and at this same hour. This second horse also contradicts the statement in line 2, "nul n'a jamais vu," and the paradox likewise collapses the twenty thousand centuries into a single instant and turns two horses into one.

It is not, however, the gesture that creates the apparition; that is, a horse turning his head in this precise manner is not what magically brings about this condensation of time. For, as the last stanza asserts, what the horse has seen will not be seen for a long while, not by "man, horse, fish or insect." This last catalogue, like that of the second stanza, is an act of diminishing (here, a descent down the phylogenetic scale) to perceivers more and more remote from man. The same act of diminishing follows, on a different plane, in the last three lines of the poem: the earth is diminished to the level of an archeological find, a once-whole statue reduced to a fragmentary relic. In a way, then, the instant of the present horse's movement lies at the apogee of time's curve: at one point, twenty thousand centuries away, is the first horse's gesture, and at another, perhaps also twenty thousand centuries removed, is a future ruined earth, where the same movement of perception may once again occur.

What does the horse see? The poem does not give the slightest clue. What it does, however, is to state an emphasis, to insist that the act of perceiving is more important than the offstage enigma. After all, the title of the poem is not "Apparition" but "Mouvement," and it is ultimately on the gesture of the poem that our attention must rest. Here, as with any Symbolist poem, we find, not a solution to the poem's mysteries but a means of embracing them and, in that, ordering them. Of the vast world traced by the poem—one which takes in all creatures, the whole earth, and millions of years—a supremely natural, insignificant turn of the head lies at the very center. The mysterious references which surround it—the eucalyptus, the "souvenir de vent," the illogical "aperçut à cette heure-ci," and the poem's strange insistence on a shattered world in the last (and, emphatically, extra) line ("Sans bras, sans jambes et sans tête")—all these only underscore the poem's main gesture. A turn of the head delineates the limits of earth's time and space. It is at once completely abstract (not even the thing seen, the object of the movement, is known), and yet completely of this world, the most normal and unnoticeable of acts. The poem, then, is a statement of the cosmic significance of this smallest of things. No one is capable of saying precisely what is so important about a turn of the head; the poem's mysteriousness is an assertion of our incapability to do so.

The persistence of the techniques of Symbolism in modern poetry cannot be demonstrated by analyzing three poems, but it is nonetheless a fact. There is nothing atypical about the three poems examined. For Mandel'štam's "Sisters" might have been substituted "Slate Ode" or "The Horse-shoe Finder"; for Crane's "Black Tambourine," "Praise for an Urn" or "The Broken Tower"; for Supervielle's "Mouve-ment," "Voyages" or "Sans-Dieu." And the same point might have been made with other poets—Pasternak or Stevens or St. John Perse. But anyone familiar with mod-ern poetry has no need of illustrations. If the Symbolists were the first poets systematically to use the structures and techniques of strangeness, they were not the last.

This is not to say, of course, that modern poetry has been an uninterrupted series of Symbolist poems written under other names; for, clearly, there are many great modern poems that have nothing to do with the Symbolists and their techniques. Rather, in pointing to Symbolist devices in modern writing we are indicating, not the continuance of the Symbolist movement, but some sort of more basic persistence, a ground relationship between Symbolism and Modernism. It makes of Mandel'štam, Crane, and Supervielle not strange throwbacks to another era but representatives of the change Symbolism has brought about in modern poetry. They show the extent to which Symbolism has been absorbed by Mod-ernism and has become a part of the landscape.

To remark on the persistence of the Symbolists' strange-ness after Symbolism's death is one thing: to explain it is quite another. For if there is some significance (as I have suggested) in the parallel between the strangeness of Sym-bolist poetry and the "strangeness" felt by the Symbolists in their relationship to their immediate world and its accepted tastes—then when the latter has disappeared (as it had in the Mandel'štam-Supervielle-Crane generation), why should the former remain?

The paradox can be partly resolved by a clear understand-ing of what the Symbolists' successors were actually saying about them. To begin with, the new poets were very natu-rally inclined to overstate their case: any poet but the most unashamed imitator is more likely to stress the differences between himself and his predecessors than to point up the similarities, precisely because he feels that what is new in him is what should attract public attention to his writing. Furthermore, he and his contemporaries are more likely to notice changes in literary norms than to notice the norms themselves: they are a "given." In other words, while the orientation of the post-Symbolist generation may have been different in some ways from that of their predecessors, it was by no means directly opposed to Symbolism.

Realizing this, some critics today pay little heed to the disclaimers of Crane and his contemporaries, and stress the aesthetic continuity between the Symbolists and the "moderns." [13] Irving Howe, in his article "The Idea of the Modern," [14] lists nine areas in which the two generations come together and sees these as comprising a Modernist aesthetic common to both. Other critics, in attempting to distinguish the Modernists from the Symbolists, speak only of differences of degree or of carrying an attitude to its extreme, rather than of basic aesthetic changes. Thus Roman Jakobson depicts the difference between the Russian Symbolists and their Modernist (Futurist, Acmeist) followers in the latters' methodical, almost scientific pursuit of the effects first hit upon by the Symbolists: it was not rare, he notes, for a Modernist poet to consult with the Moscow Linguistics Circle the way one consults a doctor for a checkup.[15] Yet, for all this methodical eccentricity, Modernism, in Jakobson's view, grows right out of Symbolism.

Implicit in all such views, and brilliantly explicit in a study by Renato Poggioli,[16] is the notion that poetry, since the mid-nineteenth century, has been a series of one avant-

13. One such study has already been mentioned: Balakian's *The Literary Origins of Surrealism*.
14. Reprinted in Howe, ed., *Literary Modernism*, pp. 11-40.
15. Roman Jakobson, "Russian Experimental Poetry of the Twentieth Century," unpubl. lecture series, Yale University, 1967.
16. *Theory of the Avant-Garde*.

garde movement after another. In other words, our idea of what a poet is underwent a significant change with the end of Romanticism, and all poets since that time (starting with the Symbolists) have been living a new role, that of the avant-garde artist.

Whereas the Romantic poet lived in Vigny's *tour d'ivoire,* the avant-garde found his dwelling transformed into the *tour abolie* of Nerval, a crumbling, shadowy relic on the outskirts of town. The poet as visionary and prophet was now dispossessed—*desdichado*—and his magnificent vantage point no longer mattered as much. The prophet became an enthusiast, his message dim or wild, and the enthusiast was secularized into protester (Dada, Surrealism, Futurism, etc.) or calmed into a mellow muser. In either case, his place is on society's periphery, for the avant-garde is just that—a vanguard, ahead of, or at least away from, the main body. To such an avant-garde artist, a poetry of strangeness will correspond as directly and forcefully to his vision of society as it did to the first *avant-gardistes,* the Symbolists.

There is, however, a more basic reason for the survival of Symbolist strangeness. It is, as I have suggested, that the historical advent of Symbolism broadened the scope of poetry's possibilities. The fact is that Symbolism *happened,* and that the first appearance of a poetry of strangeness has meant something to poetry ever since. In the Symbolists' own estimates of what they had accomplished—"rendre l'initiative aux mots" or "reprendre à la Musique leur bien" —overstated as they may be, there is a grain of truth. For with its goal of mystery, of implying withheld information, Symbolism created wholly new effects in poetry and, in its brief history, managed to broaden the reader's expectations in regard to poetry. In changing expectations it opened up possibilities for the same techniques of strangeness in modern verse.

These new possibilities define what poetry is today for every artist, whether it is true or not that he is by definition an avant-gardist. Symbolism has become the property of everyone who writes; Bob Dylan, although he may not have read Maeterlinck, has clearly inherited a poetry which Maeterlinck helped to shape.

To delight in mystery is the lesson the Symbolists taught poetry, to make strangeness reason enough for writing. If this lesson was prompted by historical circumstances that no longer prevail for all poets, there should be no paradox in its survival: there is nothing unusual in art about techniques that outlive the problem they were initially devised to solve. We know, for example, that nineteenth-century painting at one point felt "threatened" by the development of photography; and we can see, in Impressionism, what must have appeared to the nineteenth century as a possible "resolution" to the threat. No one disputes the fact that the turn taken by Impressionist painting changed the very concept of painting, and thus left its mark even on the artists of today. Yet few would claim that the photograph's initial threat is still in force or that contemporary painters are still working in reaction against it. We recognize that Impressionism changed the course of painting and that its lessons have become incorporated into our notion of the art; and this, it seems, has also been the case with Symbolism in the history of poetry.

Bibliography

Principal Sources

Aish, D. A. K. *La Métaphore dans l'œuvre de S. Mallarmé.* Paris, 1938.

Bachchan, H. R. *W. B. Yeats and Occultism.* Delhi, 1965.

Balakian, Anna. *The Literary Origins of Surrealism.* 2d ed. New York, 1966.

Belinskij, V. G. *O Klassikax Russkoj Literatury.* Moscow, 1958.

―――. *Selected Philosophical Works.* Moscow, 1956.

Belyj, Andrej. *Simvolizm.* Moscow, 1910.

―――. *Stixotvorenija i Po'emy.* Moscow, 1966.

―――. *Vospominanija ob A. Bloke.* Letchworth, Eng., 1964.

Blok, Aleksandr. "O Sovremennom Sostojanii Russkovo Simvolizma." *Apollon,* (May–June 1910), pp. 21-30.

Briant, Th. *Saint-Pol-Roux.* Paris, 1952.

Brjusov, Valerij. *Dnevniki, 1891–1910.* Moscow, 1927.

Brower, R. A. *Fields of Light.* New York, 1951.

Claudel, Paul. *Art poétique.* Paris, 1903.

Cornell, Kenneth. *The Post-Symbolist Period.* New Haven, 1958.

―――. *The Symbolist Movement.* New Haven, 1951.

Crane, Hart. *Complete Poems and Selected Letters and Prose.* Edited by Brom Weber. New York, 1966.

―――. *The Letters of Hart Crane.* Edited by Brom Weber. New York, 1952.

Décaudin, Michel. *Crise des valeurs symbolistes.* Paris, 1956.

Delbouille, Pierre. *Poésie et sonorité.* Brussels, 1965.

Dembo, L. S. *Hart Crane's Sanskrit Charge.* Ithaca, N.Y., 1960.

Eliade, M. *The Sacred and the Profane.* New York, 1959.

Ellis' (Kobylinskij). *Russkie Simvolisty.* Moscow, 1910.

Engelberg, Edward. *The Symbolist Poem.* New York, 1967.

Erlich, Victor. *Russian Formalism.* 2d ed. The Hague, 1965.

Friedrich, Hugo. *Die Struktur der modernen Lyrik.* Hamburg, 1956.

Frye, Northrop. "Three Meanings of Symbolism." *Yale French Studies,* no. 9 (Spring 1952), pp. 11-18.

Ghil, René. *Traité du Verbe.* Paris, 1886.

Ginzburg, Lidija. *O Lirike.* Moscow, 1964.

Gourmont, Rémy de. *Le Livre des masques.* Paris, 1896.

Gumilëv, Nikolai. "Nasledie simvolizma i akmeizm." *Apollon* (January 1913), pp. 42-45.

———. "Žižn stixa." *Apollon* (April 1910), pp. 5-14.

Hackett, C. A. *Modern French Poetry (from Baudelaire to the Present Day).* New York, 1963.

Hazo, Samuel. *Hart Crane.* New York, 1963.

Howe, Irving. *Literary Modernism.* New York, 1967.

Ivanov, Vj. *Svet večernij.* Edited by C. M. Bowra. London, 1962.

———. "Zavety Simvolizma." *Apollon* (May–June 1910), pp. 5–20.

Johansen, Sv. *Le Symbolisme.* Copenhagen, 1945.

Kahn, Gustave. *Premiers Poèmes.* Paris, 1897.

Lautréamont, le Comte de (Isidore Ducasse). *Œuvres complètes.* Paris, 1963.

Le Braz, Anatole. *La Légende de la mort chez les Bretons armoricains.* 2d ed. Paris, 1966.

———. *Théâtre celtique.* Paris, 1904.

Lehmann, A. G. *The Symbolist Aesthetic in France, 1885–1895.* Oxford, 1950.

Lévi, Eliphas (Alphonse-Louis Constant). *Dogme et rituel de la haute magie.* Paris, 1862.

Lewis, R. W. B. *The Poetry of Hart Crane.* New Haven, 1967.

Maeterlinck, Maurice. *Poésies complètes.* Edited by J. Hanse. Brussels, 1965.

Mallarmé, Stéphane. *Œuvres complètes.* Edited by H. Mondor. Paris, 1945.

Mandel'štam, Osip. *Sobranie Sočinenij.* 2 vols. New York, 1966.

Markov, Vl. *The Longer Poems of Velimir Khlebnikov.* Berkeley, 1962.

Markov, Vl. and M. Sparks. *Modern Russian Poetry.* New York, 1967.

Matlaw, R. E. *Belinsky, Chernyshevsky and Dobroliubov.* New York, 1962.

Mauclair, Camille. "Jules Laforgue." *Mercure de France* 17 (February–March 1896): 159-78, 302-27.

Merrill, Stuart. *Prose et vers.* Paris, 1925.

Michaud, Guy. *La Doctrine symboliste (Documents).* Paris, 1947.

———. *Message poétique du symbolisme.* 3 vols. Paris, 1947.

Mirsky, D. S. *Contemporary Russian Literature.* New York, 1926.

Moréas, Jean. *Choix de poèmes.* Paris, 1923.

Nerval, Gérard de. *Œuvres.* Edited by H. Lemaître. 2 vols. Paris, 1966.

Otto, Rudolf. *The Idea of the Holy.* London, 1929.

Panofsky, Erwin. *Studies in Iconology.* New York, 1939.

Poggioli, Renato. *Poets of Russia.* Cambridge, Mass., 1960.

—————. *The Theory of the Avant-Garde.* Cambridge, Mass., 1968.

Praz, Mario. *The Romantic Agony.* New York, 1954.

Propp, V. *Morfologia Skazki.* Leningrad, 1928.

Ramsey, Warren. *Jules Laforgue and the Ironic Inheritance.* New York, 1953.

Raymond, Marcel. *From Baudelaire to Surrealism.* 2d Eng. ed. New York, 1950.

Reeve, F. D. *Aleksandr Blok: Between Image and Idea.* New York, 1962.

Rimbaud, Arthur. *Œuvres Complètes,* Edited by Suzanne Bernard. Paris, 1960.

Schuré, Edouard. *Les Grands Initiés.* Paris, 1914.

Seward, Barbara. *The Symbolic Rose.* New York, 1960.

Signoret, Emmanuel. "Première Lettre sur la poésie." *Mercure de France,* 17 (January 1896): 29-36.

Šklovskij, Viktor. "Iskusstvo kak priëm." *Po'etika: sborniki po teorii po'etičeskovo jazyka.* Petrograd, 1919.

Slonim, Marc. *Modern Russian Literature.* New York, 1953.

Sologub, F. (F. Teternikov). *Mel'kij bes'.* English translation: *The Little Demon.* London, 1915.

—————. *Sobrannie Sočinenija.* St. Petersburg, 1909.

Solovëv, V1. *Crise de la philosophie occidentale.* Translated with an introduction by M. Herman. Paris, 1947.

Souza, R. de. *Où Nous en sommes.* Paris, 1906.

Stepun, Fedor. *Mystische Weltschau.* Munich, 1964.

Stevens, Wallace. *Poems.* New York, 1959.

—————. *The Necessary Angel.* New York, 1965.

Supervielle, Jules. "En Songeant à un Art poétique." In his *Naissances* (Paris, 1951), pp. 57-71.

—————. *Gravitations.* Paris, 1966.

Symons, Arthur. *The Symbolist Movement in Literature.* 4th ed. New York, 1958.

Taupin, René. *l'Influence du symbolisme français sur la poésie américaine.* Paris, 1929.

Thibaudet, Albert. *La Poésie de Stéphane Mallarmé.* 2d ed. Paris, 1926.

Verhaeren, Emile. *Choix de Poémes.* Paris, 1916.

Viélé-Griffin, Francis. "La Poétique nouvelle." *Mercure de France,* 16 (October 1895): 1-9.

Villiers de l'Isle-Adam P.-A. *Contes cruels.* 2d ed. Paris, 1963.

Vološin, M. "Henri de Régnier," *Apollon* (January 1910), pp. 18-34.

Wellek, René. *A History of Modern Criticism.* 4 vols. New Haven, 1965.

Wellek, René and Austin Warren. *Theory of Literature.* 3d. ed. New York, 1956.

Wilson, Edmund. *Axel's Castle.* New York, 1931.

Wimsatt, W. K. *Hateful Contraries.* Lexington, Ky., 1966.

Žirmunskij, V. *Voprosy Teorii Literatury.* Leningrad, 1928.

Other Sources

Balakian, Anna. *The Symbolist Movement.* New York, 1967.

Bally, Charles. *Traité de stylistique française.* Heidelberg, 1909.

Barre, André. *Le Symbolisme.* Paris, 1911.

Béguin, Albert. *L'Ame romantique et le rêve.* 2 vols. Paris, 1946.

Blackmur, R. P. *Language as Gesture.* New York, 1952.

Bonneau, G. *Le Symbolisme dans la poésie française contemporaine.* Paris, 1930.

Bowra, C. M. *The Heritage of Symbolism.* New York, 1961.

Brémond, (Abbé) Henri. *Prière et poésie.* Paris, 1926.

Brooks, Cleanth. *Modern Poetry and the Tradition.* New York, 1965.

Brown, Clarence. *The Prose of Osip Mandelstam.* Princeton, N.J., 1965.

Cazamian, Louis. *Symbolisme et poésie.* Neuchâtel, Switzerland, 1947.

Champigny, R. "Situation de Jules Laforgue." *Yale French Studies,* no. 9 (Spring 1952).

Charpentier, John. *Le Symbolisme.* Paris, 1927.

Charpier, Jacques. *Saint-John Perse.* Paris, 1962.

Chiari, Joseph. *Symbolisme from Poe to Mallarmé.* New York, 1956.

Coléno, Pierre. *Portes d'ivoire.* Paris, 1948.

Donchin, Georgette. *The Influence of French Symbolism on Russian Poetry*. The Hague, 1958.
———. "A Russian Symbolist Journal." *RLC* 30:405-20.
Eliot, T. S. *From Poe to Valéry*. New York, 1948.
Empson, William. *Seven Types of Ambiguity*. 3d ed. New York, 1955.
Erlich, Victor. *The Double Image*. Baltimore, 1964.
Estève, Cl.-L. *Etudes philosophiques sur l'expression littéraire*. Paris, 1938.
Etiemble. *Le Mythe de Rimbaud*. 3 vols. Paris, 1961.
———. *Supervielle*. Paris, 1960.
Feidelson, Charles. *Symbolism and American Literature*. Chicago, 1953.
Fiser, Emérie. *Le Symbole littéraire*. Paris, 1941.
Fowlie, Wallace. "The Legacy of Symbolism." *Yale French Studies*, no. 9 (Spring 1952), 20-26.
Freeman, Ralph. "Symbol as Terminus: Some Notes on Symbolist Narrative." *Comparative Literature Studies* 4 (January–February 1967), pp. 135-45.
Frey, J. A. *Motif Symbolism in the Disciples of Mallarmé*. Washington, D.C., 1957.
Frye, Northrop. *Sound and Poetry*. New York, 1957.
Gengoux, Jacques. *Le Symbolisme de Mallarmé*. Paris, 1950.
Ghil, René. *Les Dates et les Œuvres*. Paris, 1923.
Greene, Tatiana. *Jules Supervielle*. Paris, 1958.
Guiraud, Pierre. *La Stylistique*. Paris, 1954.
———. "Tendencies de la stylistique contemporaine." In his *Style et littérature*. The Hague, 1962.
Hatzfield, H. "The Language of Symbolist Poets." *Studies in Philology* 43:93.
Hiddleston, J. A. *l'Univers de Jules Supervielle*. Paris, 1965.
Horton, Phillip. *Hart Crane*. New York, 1937.
Kahn, Gustave. *Symbolistes et décadents*. Paris, 1902.
Levin, Harry. *Contexts of Criticism*. Cambridge, Mass., 1958.
MacIntyre, C. F. *French Symbolist Poetry*. Berkeley, 1958.
Martino, Pierre. *Parnasse et symbolisme*. Paris, 1935.
Maslenikov, Oleg. *Frenzied Poets: André Biely and the Russian Symbolists*. Berkeley, 1952.
Mirsky, D. S. *History of Russian Literature*. Edited by F. J. Whitfield. New York, 1958.

116

Morice, Charles. *La Littérature de tout à l'heure*. Paris, 1889.
Noulet, E. *Etudes littéraires*. Mexico City, 1944.
Otsup, Nikolai. *Sovremenniki*. Paris, 1961.
Pucciani, O. "The Universal Language of Symbolism." *Yale French Studies* no. 9 (Spring 1952), p. 27.
Quinn, Vincent. *Hart Crane*. New York, 1963.
Ragusa, Olga. *Mallarmé in Italy*. New York, 1957.
Ramsey, Warren. "American Imagism, French Symbolism." *Comparative Literature Studies* 4 (January–February 1967): pp. 177-93.
Roy, Claude. *Jules Superveille*. Paris, 1964.
Royère, Jean. *Mallarmé*. Paris, 1931.
Seboek, T. A. *Style in Language*. Cambridge, Mass., 1964.
Sénéchal, Christian. *Jules Supervielle*. Paris, 1939.
Slonim, Marc. *Soviet Russian Literature*. Oxford, 1964.
Smith, Horatio E. *Columbia Dictionary of Modern European Literature*. New York, 1947.
Struve, Gleb. *Russkaja Literatura v Izgnanii*. New York, 1956.
Tate, Allen. *Forlorn Demon*. New York, 1953.
———. *The Language of Poetry*. New York, 1960.
Temple, Ruth Z. *Critic's Alchemy, A Study of the Introduction of French Symbolism into England*. New York, 1953.
Tindall, W. Y. *The Literary Symbol*. New York, 1955.
Todarov, Tz. *Théorie de la littérature*. Paris, 1966.
Trahard, Pierre. *Le Mystère poétique*. Paris, 1940.
Valéry, Paul. *Œuvres complètes*. Paris, 1965.
Vat, D. G. *The Fabulous Opera*. Groningen-Batavia, 1936.
Voekler, Hunce. *The Hart Crane Voyages*. New York, 1967.
Weinberg, Bernard. *The Limits of Symbolism*. Chicago, 1966.
Wheelwright, Phillip. *Metaphor and Reality*. Bloomington, Ind., 1962.
Wimsatt, W. K. *The Verbal Icon*. New York, 1965.
Zumthor, P. "Stylistique et poétique." In his *Style et Littérature*, pp. 25-38. The Hague, 1962.

Index